WORLD WAR II
FROM MY POINT OF VIEW

WORLD WAR II
FROM MY POINT OF VIEW

by

T/117503 - DRIVER A. O. BENNION

ROYAL ARMY SERVICE CORPS

Avon Books
1 Dovedale Studios, 465 Battersea Park Road,
London SW11 4LR

Printed and bound in the U.K.

Avon Books

London
First Published 1998
© A. O. Bennion, 1998
ISBN 1 86033 511 X

DEDICATED TO
SHEILA

A. O. BENNION

CONTENTS

Chapter III

AFRICA - TUNISIA - SICILY - ITALY
APRIL 1943 TO DECEMBER 1945

LIST OF ILLUSTRATIONS

PREFACE

My father served in the Royal Artillery throughout the Great War of 1914 to 1918, and when my wife and I were having lunch with our son Michael, he happened to mention that he had never managed to find out from his grandfather what life in the Army was like in those dreadful days. When I casually mentioned that I still had all my War diaries covering my own time in the army in World War II, Michael immediately said that he would be interested to read them. This was quite impossible, as they were scribbled in fourteen small notebooks, and in any case my handwriting is almost illegible to anyone except myself (and even to me sometimes). However I said I would try to summarise them for him. Once I had started I got rather carried away, and this is the result.

I have tried to convey the atmosphere and camaraderie that prevailed during those years and I can only hope that the reader will enjoy reading about it as much as I enjoyed the writing.

1996

CHAPTER 1

ENGLAND - FRANCE - BELGIUM
September 1939 to June 1940

I enlisted with Duncan, my future brother-in-law, on Friday, September 15th 1939, in the Royal Army Service Corps (RASC), one of the few branches of the Service that was still accepting volunteers in those early days of the war. By signing on at the same time we hoped we might stay together for our initial training and perhaps be drafted into the same unit. ('The best laid plans o' mice and men'). Although we were now officially in the Army, we were not required to report until Wednesday, the 20th, so we had a few days for preparation and farewells, especially as the 15th had been my parents' Silver Wedding Anniversary. We duly reported at the local Institute and were given Railway Warrants and travelled by train from New Street Station, Birmingham, to Aldershot. There were about a dozen of us and we were met at Aldershot Station by a corporal with an Army coach that took us to Buller Barracks on the main Aldershot camp. After a meal we were taken to our barrack room where we would be sleeping and were then free till 'lights out' at 10.30. Duncan and I took a walk into Aldershot but returned and turned in early after a somewhat traumatic day.

Next morning after breakfast we were told to parade on the main parade ground, about two hundred of us. A sergeant took a roll call and then said (or rather shouted) that the men whose names he would call out were to fall out and assemble separately. My name was called, but not Duncan's. By the time this segregation was completed our parade numbered about a hundred and we were told to collect all our belongings from the barracks and report back in half an hour. I then realised that we were about to be moved, so I approached the sergeant and explained Duncan's and my position, but he said there was nothing he could do; so, at the risk of life and limb, I managed to sneak up to Duncan, who was still on parade, for a quick handshake and 'best of luck'. I was not to see him again until 1946 after the end of the war. On reporting back on the parade ground with our belongings we were transported by coach back to Aldershot Station where we boarded a special troop train and learnt that our destination was Southport.

We arrived in the late afternoon and after a meal in the Territorial Army Barracks we were allotted civilian billets, as our barracks were not yet ready. Next morning we were collected and again paraded outside a drill hall and told a bit more about the reason for our sudden move from Aldershot. Apparently it had been decreed by 'top brass' in Whitehall that infantry should not be expected to march long distances and then go straight into action. Therefore new transport units were being formed to carry the infantry and their kit forward to the front line so that they would go into action comparatively fresh. These new companies were to be called 'Troop Carrying Coys' and were being formed from basic Territorial units (in our case the West Lancs with the red rose emblem), but augmented by volunteer drivers brought in from Aldershot. We were to be No. 3 Company and would comprise two thirds 'Terriers' and one third volunteers. Most of the men from Aldershot had enlisted as HGV drivers. Here I should mention that in the RASC the term 'driver' is an actual rank, the equivalent of Private in the Infantry and sapper in the Engineers. Whilst on the subject of rank, I should explain about motor cyclists. In a transport unit such as ours motorcycles play an integral part - in our unit there were about thirty motor cyclists, and that is their rank. The popular term 'Despatch Rider' is used exclusively by the Royal Corps of Signals.

Although the actual composition of the new units did not emerge till later, it is perhaps relevant to describe them here. Each Company would consist of five Platoons, a Headquarters, a Workshop and three working platoons. Taking personnel first; Headquarters consisted of the Commanding Officer (a Major),

Adjutant (a 2/Lieut.), Sergeant Major, Quartermaster Sergeant, one Sergeant, two corporals, two batmen drivers, two motor cyclists, a CSM clerk, a Company Orderly, and about forty other ranks, for cooks, clerks, guards, fatigues etc. Workshop Platoon was commanded by a Captain, one MSM (Mechanist Sergeant Major) a Staff Sergeant, two corporal clerks, one batman and about two dozen qualified mechanics and fitters. Each of the three platoons (A, B & C) was commanded by a Captain with a 2/Lieut. as second-in-command, five corporals, five lance-corporals, two motor cyclists, two batmen and about fifty drivers. This gives a total for the company of about 300 men. Vehicles were as follows:- Headquarters, Major's staff car, (A Humber Snipe), Adjutant's car (a Ford 10) three Bedford three-tonners, one 15 cwt. pick-up, one water tanker and four motor cycles (Matchless 350 cc.). Workshop platoon comprised a Vauxhall 12 for the Captain, two specially fitted out workshop vehicles complete with power drills, lathes, grinders etc., four Bedford three-tonners for spares, tyres, etc., one 15 cwt, pick-up, one water tanker and two motor cycles. Each working platoon had a Vauxhall 12 for the Captain, a Ford 10 for the 2/Lt., 28 Bedford three-tonners, one 15 cwt. pick-up, one water tanker and eight motor cycles. This gives a total for the unit of about 150 vehicles.

Back to Saturday September 23rd and our second day at Southport. First we were issued with our uniform and kit (but no rifles as, in those early days of the war, they were still in short supply). We were also given paper and string to wrap up our 'civvie' clothing for posting home. Next the Aldershot intake were allotted their duties. All the officers and NCOs were 'Terriers' whose duties were already allocated. I had learnt on the 'grapevine' that if you could get the magic letters R/E (Regimentally Employed) after your name on the Regimental Roll, you were automatically exempt from all guard duties and fatigues, the bane of every soldier's life: so when the position of Company Orderly came up for allocation I quickly stepped forward and was given the 'job'. Nobody seemed to know what my duties were, but I was in HQ platoon and R/E, which was all that mattered at that moment. Most of the rest of the Aldershot contingent were allocated as drivers in the three working platoons. We were also told that, following a short period of intensive training, the unit would be going overseas. The next few weeks passed all too swiftly - I managed an unofficial weekend leave on October 7th and 8th and an official one on October 14th and 15th. We marched and drilled incessantly and gradually got used to the heavy army boots, which cut into your ankles. I eased mine by daring to make half inch cuts round the tops, fortunately hidden by the webbing gaiters which had now replaced the old puttees of the last war. Groups of drivers went down to Bedford and Luton to collect our trucks and cars and our motor cycles arrived in the back of lorries.

A brief description of the Bedford 3-tonners, as these were the workhorses of the unit. They were standard open trucks, but camouflage painted and fitted with a simple bench down each side for the Infantry to sit on, with their kit piled down the centre and a let-down back. They had wooden hoops that fitted into slots outside the low sides, over which a large tarpaulin could be stretched. Each truck could carry 20 men, ten down each side, so each platoon could lift 500 men at a time and the whole unit up to 1500 men and equipment. The tarpaulin was partly to give shelter to the infantry but also acted as additional camouflage. Each truck also had a large camouflage net that could be quickly stretched out to cover the whole vehicle. Headlights were fitted with a mask with a narrow slot, giving very little forward light. Rear and brake lights had been removed, but the differential casing under the rear was painted with glossy white paint with a small light fitting shining on it for use in night driving convoys.

At the end of October we were given three days embarkation leave from the 20th to the 22nd, and the entire unit left Southport in convoy on Wednesday, the 25th, arriving at Newport Docks in S. Wales the following day. Here we were separated from our vehicles which would be following in a slower cargo ship, and on Sunday the 29th we went on board the *Lady of Mann*, a ferry that used to ply the Irish Sea route between Liverpool and Belfast. We learnt that, as she was quite fast, we would be making the crossing with just one destroyer escort. Here I must mention one incredible coincidence - when I was due to come home in December 1945 at the end of the war and arrived at Calais from Italy, there was the same old *Lady of Mann* waiting to take me home. Somehow she had survived six years of warfare.

We docked at St Nazaire on the west coast of France, on

Wednesday, November 1st, after a pretty rough crossing of the Bay of Biscay. Before leaving Newport I had enjoyed a meal of biscuits and sardines, but regretted it later and 'lost' it all somewhere off France. Our vehicles arrived a couple of days later and we proceeded in convoy across France. A few days were spent at Le Mans, where the trucks' superstructures and tarpaulins were refitted (they had been removed for the sea crossing). One job that fell to me and a few others was the stamping of identity discs. Every man had to wear two discs, one green and one red, round his neck at all times. In case of death one disc is left on the body for identification and the other sent to HQ as proof of death. The discs are made of tough plastic and have the owner's name, rank and number stamped on. As the unit had been formed in such a hurry these had never been completed before we left England, but it now became a top priority; so a few of us spent hours with the nominal roll, hammers and a set of metal punches stamping out discs - you can imagine the time it took - every letter and figure had to be stamped individually.

Our route eastward across France took five days, stopping at Airiaignes on Nov. 8th, Monchy-au-Bois on the 9th, and Lievins on the 10th. We stayed here for three weeks and finally arrived at our destination near the Belgium frontier on the 29th. This was to be our 'home base' for the next few months. The village was called Authieulle.

When the company is on the move as over the past weeks an officer and a motor cyclist from each platoon go on ahead to the next destination to arrange accommodation, parking areas for the vehicles, sites for cookhouses, messes, etc. The unit is quite self-supporting; rations are drawn daily from the nearest RASC Supply Depot and the route of the convoy is arranged so that it passes fuel dumps, where vehicles can be refuelled as necessary. When all this has been arranged, usually with the help of the local Maire of the town or village, the motor cyclist returns to the convoy to guide it to the pre-arranged site. HQ Platoon ideally needs three rooms for its headquarters, one for the CO and Adjutant, an HQ Office (Orderly Room) and one for the Company Stores. Where no rooms are available, the Orderly Room is the back of one of the 3-tonners, and the stores stay in the back of the stores truck. If we have to use the back of a truck for the office, desks are improvised by using a few planks laid across a couple of boxes with folding stools as chairs - not very comfortable, especially in the depth of winter, but manageable.

At Authieulle we were lucky. A single story cottage was requisitioned consisting of three rooms, the one on the left was the CO's and Adjutant's office, the middle one was the Orderly Room and the third the storeroom. The owner of the cottage, a farmer and his wife, lived opposite and we soon became good friends. The Orderly Room 'staff' slept in the office - we were a very close-knit little community - Cpl. Jack Armstrong, the company clerk, Cpl, Knibbs (known as 'Nibby'), Jack Browne, the CSM's clerk and my particular pal, self as Company Orderly, and 'Titch' Derby, the motor cyclist. (He was a brilliant rider having owned a 1000cc Norton in 'civvie' street, so his 350cc Matchless was a bit of a come-down). There was also the three platoon clerks, Tom Whitby, a charming chap who used to be with the AA, Alistair McWhinnie, a Scot, and Freddie Pilling, a huge man, a grown-up Billy Bunter with a round chubby face and always smiling. All these were 'Terriers', myself being the only Aldershot intake.

During the day the Orderly Room was the company office with trestle tables, chairs, filing cabinets, typewriters, etc. But after the orderly room 'closed' it became our recreation room and sleeping quarters. I commandeered a pool table for my 'bed', made comfortable by 'borrowing' about six blankets from the stores. The others each had their own spots, with camp beds, air pillows, etc. Our evenings were spent reading, writing letters, playing cards or going into the local village for a meal.

One officer was appointed 'Duty Officer' each day, whose job was to visit every platoon to check on vehicle guards, cookhouses, latrines, etc. He usually finished each night with a visit to the orderly room for a cup of tea and a chat. If any messages arrived when the orderly room was 'closed', Titch took them to the Officers' Mess, but this rarely happened during these first stagnant months of the war.

Our daily routine was very relaxed - we got up about eight o'clock, cleared away our sleeping paraphernalia, and went across to the farmhouse for a wash and shave (in hot water) - then breakfast with the farmer and his wife in their warm kitchen - this was usually rolls, jam and coffee. Then back across the road to the orderly room about nine, when the officers and sergeant major arrived. There were constant comings and goings all day, platoon officers, motor cyclists, visiting officers etc. Even on active service it is surprising how much paperwork has to be done - nominal rolls kept up to date, movement orders, duty rosters, indents for stores, vehicle registers, vehicle accident reports, men and vehicle availability to GHQ, etc. etc. We each had our different duties. Jack (CSM's clerk) typed out daily Part II orders for the unit giving details of new instructions, parades, and all the information that needed to be passed down from HQ to the platoons. My own particular job (that I think I never finished) was amending King's Regulations. This is the Army 'Bible' and covers every eventuality that can possibly befall a unit on active service. It was a thick paperback volume and as amendments had been received over the past months they had simply been stored away in a box. My job was to cut out the amendment, find the relevant passage and paste it in the book. Sometimes it was a mere word, or it could be a whole paragraph or simply a deletion. Anyway it was a tedious job, but fortunately I was on call for any other job that cropped up and any such diversion was very welcome.

Another job that fell to me was the distribution of cigarettes. I don't know if it still applies in these health-conscious days, but during World War II every soldier serving overseas was entitled to a free tin of fifty cigarettes weekly. They were collected with the rations and I had to give the platoon supply corporals their allocation. As a non-smoker, I naturally sold my tin!

We usually had our meals in the orderly room, these being brought to us in the pick-up and eaten at our 'desks'. There were several parades - the two daily ones were the morning 'sick parade', where any man could report to the orderly room at 9 o'clock and be seen by the medical orderly, who would decide if he needed to be sent to the local Medical Officer or just be dosed with a couple of pills. The other daily parade was 'Defaulters', where any man who had offended during the previous twenty-four hours was marched in front of the CO by the sergeant-major. (Another of my 'jobs' was to act as an escort to these 'prisoners'). The most usual offences were drunkenness or pilfering for which the punishment was usually extra guards or fatigues or perhaps a forfeit of so many days pay. All this helped to dispel the daily monotony.

The other two parades were weekly and these were held on a platoon basis. Pay parade was always very popular. Pay was always given out by an officer and each man had to sign to say that he had received it. Bath parades too were popular. A quota of men would be detailed to be taken to the nearest town to patronise the local public baths or showers. This usually included a certain amount of free time for shopping or having a meal in the local café.

Here I should mention letters and censorship. All letters leaving the unit had to be censored by an officer, one of their most tedious and distasteful duties, though how meticulously they did it is uncertain. All outgoing letters had to be placed, unsealed in the platoon box. After scrutiny the officer would countersign the letter, seal the envelope, to be taken by the post corporal to the local Army Post office, where he would pick up any incoming mail. There was one exception to this unit censorship. Special 'Green Envelopes' (so called because the printing on the outside was green) were issued on the basis of one per man per week. (Another of my duties). On the outside of the envelope was a certificate that had to be signed by the sender stating that the letter contained only personal and private matters. These could be sealed and taken straight to the A.P.O. They were liable to base censorship, but, as the writer would be unknown to the officer, it was much more acceptable than unit censorship. Johnnie Williams drove the HQ pick-up and was i/c post and was probably the most popular man in the unit. He also 'resided' in the orderly room. There was one breach of censorship when one corporal Sandy, a very educated and intelligent lad and quite a good artist, sketched the view from his window and cleverly incorporated the name of the village where we were billeted into a hedge. It got past the unit censor, but was picked up by base censor, who returned it to our CO for 'appropriate action'. I remember he was brought up before the CO, but as I recall, he got off quite lightly, but it caused quite a stir at the time.

One of the main problems during this period of inactivity was boredom - vehicle maintenance occupied most of the men's time, but as the trucks were doing very little mileage there was little to do, apart from the regular workshop service, which was very rigid. A few of us would go into the local town some evenings for a visit to the local cinema and a meal in a café, usually eggs, chips and beans. One day Jack and I decided to treat ourselves to the luxury of a shave - it was miserable weather, wet and snowing. We found a barber's shop and on going in found to our surprise that the barber was a lady. She intimated that her husband was in the army and she was trying to keep the business going. She gave us a very professional shave, which was very welcome.

One of the advantages of being in a unit such as ours was that there was never any shortage of transport - we could always 'lay on' or 'borrow' a truck or bike or persuade Johnnie to take us in his 15 cwt. and pick us up later - we never walked anywhere. We also organised some impromptu inter-platoon hockey matches, which the combined officers and sergeants messes usually managed to win, probably for diplomatic reasons!

One essential in any transport unit was maps - of course at this time there was no such thing as mobile phones and we had no means of communication by radio; so all messages had to be by word of mouth or written. All locations were identified either by village name or map reference, so maps were widely distributed - every officer, NCO and motor cyclist had a complete set.

The weather during this winter was particularly severe with heavy snowfalls followed by floods. General health was not too bad; colds, sore throats, minor accidents, most of which were treated by our medical orderly, but one lad had to go into the Field Hospital suffering from double pneumonia. I suppose the worst aspect was a feeling of general depression, due partly to being away from home and loved ones and the prolonged inactivity - this was not what we had joined up for.

Perhaps here I should describe how we obtained what was our 'life blood', i.e. petrol. All vehicles were always kept with full tanks and carried two 5 gallon spares. Fuel was obtained from huge supply dumps of containers, of which there were two types - first the 'Jerrican', a stout metal container holding 5 gallons with a hinged sealed lid, which were the type carried as spares. The other type was a very flimsy canister made of thin tinfoil, about 18 inches high and about ten inches square. These were very vulnerable and the metal was very thin and easily punctured. To empty one simply punched a hole in a corner and, when empty, threw it away. Being so thin one always found empty cans in the dump, where the tin had been accidentally pierced and the petrol just drained away. The wastage must have been terrible, but of course they were much cheaper to produce and were expendable.

Perhaps here I should explain why we were 'stuck' here on the Franco/Belgian frontier for these long winter months. After the last war the Belgian Government was terrified of becoming involved again, and counted on their strict neutrality to remain out this time. Consequently they thought that, if they kept the allies (British and French) out of their territory, the Germans would respect their neutrality. If, however, the Germans did violate their Eastern frontier then the Belgian Government would 'invite' the allies into Belgium. The Belgian army's defences along their eastern border were very limited, relying mostly on natural barriers such as canals and rivers, but of course when the invasion did eventually come, these presented little obstacles to the highly motorised and efficient German forces.

1940

On Sunday, January 14th we left Authieulle for an exercise based on Ennevelin. It lasted a week and during this time there was a great deal of practice convoy work and I found myself doing traffic-control at various cross-roads. Eventually the exercise came to an end and we returned to our base and resumed our daily routine.

About this time to our surprise the matter of leave cropped up and this began during the latter part of February and the typing of leave passes, travel warrants and instructions became another daily chore for the company orderly. From March 9th to the 13th there was another short exercise near the frontier, during which we were billeted in a chateau. On all these occasions we knew little of what was going on; we were told to report to such and such a place at a certain time and then be told what was to happen next. We were back at our base just a week before my leave was due on March 20th. On the 19th I packed up my kit for the off the next day and reported to a Rest Camp at 1.30 p.m. I and another lad from Workshops Platoon then went by train via Arras and Amiens and finally arrived at Boulogne about 5.30 p.m. We went straight aboard a ferry, the *Biarritz*, and she sailed later that night. We had a couple of fighter planes and a destroyer as escort, as we heard there was a General Ironside on board. We crossed the Channel without incident and landed at Dover early the next morning. Then a train to Birmingham and a well earned rest.

After a relaxing ten days at home I returned to the unit on April 1ˢᵗ to find things very much as when I left. The daily routine was resumed until the 28ᵗʰ, when the Major's driver, George Walker, went on leave and I took over driving his Humber, a job I had always coveted. Here I think I should be more explicit and try to reconstruct the events in chronological order as they unrolled from day to day.

April 28ᵗʰ - Sunday

Left Mercatel in the Humber with the major and followed a convoy to Cyosing where the major stayed the night and I slept in the guardroom of the 6ᵗʰ Gordons.

April 29ᵗʰ - Monday

Up at 5.30 a.m. and major led HQ platoon to join convoy to Achiet-le-Grande, where we stayed the night. We slept on the stage of a hall which was the sergeants' mess.

April 30ᵗʰ - Tuesday

Up at 7.00 a.m. and had a free morning. In the afternoon I took the major to Brigade Headquarters of No. 3 Infantry Brigade and we got back to the billet just after midnight.

May 1ˢᵗ - Wednesday

Up at 3.45 a.m. and left with the major at 5.30 with convoy to Henn - I was then free for the rest of the day.

May 2ⁿᵈ - Thursday to May 9ᵗʰ Thursday

During this week there was little activity apart from a tour of the 1914 - 1918 trenches, which was very interesting though horrific. They had been left exactly as they had been at the end of the war in 1918. We could not know that this was the end of the 'lull before the storm'.

May 10ᵗʰ - Friday

This was the day things really began to happen - the day the

Germans invaded Belgium and the day the B.E.F. and French forces went into Belgium. All the planning and practice of the previous months were put into effect. Our company was to transport the advance troops of the Third Infantry Brigade as an advance force. We were up at 6 a.m. and I drove the major with Titch to the rendezvous on the frontier, where we arrived about 9. The three platoons had already picked up the infantry. The rest of the HQ platoon arrived about 4 p.m. There were several air raids and one plane was shot down. We were issued with 50 rounds of ammo apiece and loaded our rifles. I slept with Titch in the Humber from about 10 p.m. till 2.30 a.m.

Here I will interrupt the diary and give an account of the campaign as I wrote it down immediately afterwards.

"The BEF entered Belgium on May 11th and from then to the 18th was being reinforced, but owing to the extensive use of armoured fighting vehicles by the Germans and the lack of effective anti-tank barriers or time to erect same, the BEF was unable to hold its defensive position and was compelled to withdraw. The retreat reached a climax on the night of May 18/19th, when two Troop Carrying Companies, comprising some 150 vehicles were detailed to withdraw three infantry brigades to an area west of the Franco/Belgian frontier. As only half of one company (No. 3) arrived in the first place, there were grave doubts as to whether part of the three brigades would be captured by the advancing Germans. The infantry had gone a considerable time without food and had marched 40 - 50 miles from the line to the rendezvous. Consequently they were in no condition to form an emergency defence position or to offer any serious resistance. However, by only taking the troops part of the way back and immediately returning for more, the TC vehicles that had arrived managed to withdraw nearly the whole of the two brigades. The other TCC which arrived later is presumed to have withdrawn the other brigade, but at present this is only surmise.

On the final retreat it was impossible to maintain proper convoy intervals owing to the huge numbers of vehicles withdrawing at short notice. Consequently the convoys presented an excellent target for hostile aircraft. At one point nine bombers flew over the convoy and dropped incendiary bombs, which scored direct hits on a petrol lorry and an ammunition truck, causing considerable damage and loss of life and effectively blocking the main road. Vehicles were thus forced to make lengthy detours. Twenty vehicles of 3 TCC returned to the rendezvous for a final lift of the remaining troops and crossed the frontier into France. Bridges were blown up behind the last vehicles as they crossed with the German advance guards already in sight. Thus once again Belgium is in the hands of the German Empire."

This is the end of my diary entry, so I will now revert to recording my own personal activity while all this was going on.

May 11th - Saturday

We were up at 2.30 a.m. and left with the 3rd Infantry Brigade HQ with their brigadier and escorted the convoy into Belgium at 5.35 a.m. and on to Brussels, where we got a rapturous reception - flags and bunting everywhere. After the infantry had debussed we left the area about 3.00 p.m. and returned to a monastery called 'La Tombe'(!) about 5. We slept in the monastery that night, during which there were several air raids.

May 12th - Sunday

During the day the unit picked up troops from the 1st Guards Brigade comprising men from the Coldstreams, the Hampshires and the Grenadiers. I left with the major and joined the convoy in the late afternoon and returned to Brussels where we arrived at about 8.30 p.m. There were more air raids and rumours of parachutists, though we never saw any. I was on traffic control on a cross-roads from then until 6.30 next morning, having driven about 60 miles during the day.

May 13th - Monday

After coffee and jam sandwiches we returned to Philimpin, arriving about 9.30 a.m., when there was a big air raid. This was a French area and it was an easy day after driving 120 miles.

May 14th - Tuesday

We were up at 4 a.m. and left for Brussels at 5, arriving about 10. I was on traffic control duty for the rest of the day.

May 15th - Wednesday

I was picked up by the CO at 1 a.m. and had an hour's sleep in the car. I took over driving at 2 a.m. but the car broke down and had to be towed back to the workshops by one of our recovery vehicles at about 7 a.m. There were many smashes and air raids during the morning while the car was being repaired. When it was completed I returned to HQ and had the rest of the day free. After a meal in a café with Tom and Jack we bedded down in the back of a truck.

May 16th - Thursday

Up at 8 a.m. (for a change) and had a free morning. At 12.30 I set off with the CO to Seclin and Lille with Ronnie, Ernie and Titch. I returned to HQ with messages.

May 17th - Friday

I was on traffic control again from 2 a.m. till 1p.m., when I was picked up by the Bren wagon, but I don't recall where we went. Was free for the rest of the day.

May 18th - Saturday

I was free till 6 p.m. so was able to catch up on some badly needed sleep. Although we didn't know it at the time, this was the day the Germans broke through the French lines to the south and began their swift advance westward preparatory to cutting off all the allied forces in the north. At 6 p.m., at half an hour's notice, I left with the CO and Adjutant and arrived at the rendezvous at Leuze about 9 p.m. The town was deserted, except for an anti-aircraft battery and all the buildings were demolished after heavy shelling. We learnt that there had been a massive retreat during the night. Forty vehicles from our company arrived instead of over a hundred expected to lift the infantry out - they were exhausted after a forty to fifty mile march. The rest of our company and another TCC arrived later. The infantry were loaded quickly and taken back to the debussing area and the vehicles immediately returned for another lift. At this point I will try to describe conditions prevailing during this retreat. All roads were swarming with refugees, all heading westward trying to escape the advancing Germans. Mostly they were on foot, carrying all their belongings on their backs or pulling handcarts. There were a few cars for those lucky enough to have petrol for as long as it lasted, and quite a few horses and carts. Whenever planes appeared everyone dived for the ditches and remained there till the danger was past, and then resumed their weary way. Thus any kind of convoy discipline was quite impossible and our vehicles moved as and when they could. Of course there was also a huge amount of BEF mechanised transport, artillery, Bren carriers, ambulances, staff cars and motor cyclists, all trying to make the best time under impossible conditions.

May 19th - Sunday

After a few hours sleep I was again on traffic control duty on a cross-roads most of the day. At this time we were billeted at a place called Phalempin. I left with the CO at short notice at 11 that night and after driving through the night we arrived at our destination, 'Foret de Nieppe', in France at about 7 the next morning.

May 20th - Monday

During the morning I took the CO to Bethune and while he was in conference I bought myself some food at a local café. We returned to the Foret about midday and I found that George, the CO's driver, had managed to rejoin us from leave, so he took over the Humber again and I was given a Matchless bike that workshops had been carrying as a spare, so, with Titch I became the second HQ motor cyclist. I had never ridden a motor cycle before, but with Titch's help I soon got the hang of it. (Talk about being thrown in at the deep end!!) At this time the whole company was hidden in the woods. I bedded down in the Humber that night.

May 21ˢᵗ - Tuesday

This was a fairly uneventful day. I sorted out my kit and stowed it on one of the HQ trucks and got used to my new bike. In the late afternoon I had to take a message to GHQ, where I heard that the advance German motorised units were already in Amiens and Arras. I got back to the unit about 7. There was a lot of air activity and planes machine-gunning the refugees. I bedded down in the back of a truck with George, Jack and Titch.

May 22ⁿᵈ - Wednesday

We were up at 7 and, as I was not on duty, I found myself on guard from 11 a.m. to 1 p.m. and again from 4 p.m. to 6 p.m. with Tom Clark.

May 23ʳᵈ - Thursday

We were up at 8 a.m. and left hurriedly with the Adjutant. We travelled with a convoy all day in pouring rain back into Belgium and arrived, soaking wet, at a place called Proven about 4 o'clock. We had done 112 miles and after a meal I bedded down in the back of Ben's truck.

May 24ᵗʰ - Friday

Up late about 9 and messed about all day. There were many German planes about. Jack and I walked to a Military Cemetery and then back to the woods where the unit was parked up.

May 25ᵗʰ - Saturday

We were up at 8 o'clock and at 11 that morning we had our first direct air raid. Many planes dive-bombed the woods where we were hidden, causing several casualties. The bombs were all of light calibre so the damage was relatively small, but a direct hit on a truck was enough to destroy it. I was terrified, and as we had no slit trenches or cover of any kind all we could do was to lie prone and pray. I was on duty at HQ from 2 o'clock and we had a second raid about 3. Whether they knew we were there or were just bombing at random we never knew. This time I was in the house that was our HQ so it wasn't quite so bad. At 10 o'clock that night we moved out and I was with the CO, Adjutant and Titch in convoy in heavy rain. At some point the bike broke down and I found myself stranded.

May 26ᵗʰ - Sunday

I diagnosed the bike's problem as an oiled plug and spent several hours trying to borrow a plug spanner from an artillery unit stationed nearby. I watched them 'lay' their big guns, during which there were many planes about and two were shot down. Eventually I got the bike going again and caught up with the unit at Englos near Lille. We could hear heavy bombardment in the distance. German planes were over constantly, but had other targets. Early afternoon I was attached to GHQ near Lille. While waiting orders I bought some bread, butter, cheese and biscuits. I was caught in a big air raid and had to take cover. Back at GHQ I found that they were preparing to move out and I was instructed to report back to my unit, where I arrived about 10 that night.

May 27ᵗʰ - Monday

After a short rest I left with HQ and one platoon about midnight. After escorting the convoy for some miles I was so exhausted that I had to put the bike on a truck, clambered in with it and slept until we reached our destination, Jan-de-Bixien in the early hours of the morning. After some coffee and bread and butter we rested in a barn, when there were several more air raids. I woke up to find all the lorries had left, including Ben's with all my kit. I left with Mr Wilson, one of our Lieutenants and we arrived at our old HQ in Proven woods, where I led the convoy to a new parking area. There was a heavy raid by about twelve Messerschmitts, including machine gunning. One of the HQ staff, Ronnie Moncur was hurt, though not badly. He was put in a staff car and I went with them to the First Aid Station, where he was left. On returning to the woods I found several of our lorries ablaze. I parked my bike and managed to move four of them away from the surrounding flames. On returning to collect my bike I found the truck near it was also ablaze and had to wait till it was burnt out before I could retrieve my bike. I then realised that the lost truck was the one with all my kit on it, so now I only had the possessions (including this diary) in the haversack I always carried with me. After escorting another convoy, I towed another of our motor cyclists who had broken down, to his platoon in another village. I then met up with Freddie and his supply wagon. We bought some lemonade and biscuits in a local shop and later there were more raids accompanied by heavy anti-aircraft fire. We then returned to the woods, where the remainder of the platoon was parked. Four of our lorries were abandoned and set on fire. We slept in the barn, the last real sleep I was to have for many days.

May 28th - Tuesday

This was the day that the Belgian Government surrendered to Hitler, though of course we had no knowledge of this at the time. We were up at 8.30 a.m. and after Oxo and biscuits we left with the remains of the convoy at about 11. For the past few days we had realised that the military situation had become very serious, but it was only when we reached a large field filled with vehicles of every description, that we realised how bad it really was and that we were going to be evacuated. We abandoned all our vehicles and bikes, to be blown up by the Royal Engineers later, and set off to march northwards towards the coast, about 12 miles distant, though we didn't know this at the time. We arrived at Bray Dunes, a small Belgium seaside resort about 4 p.m. Naturally it was deserted so we rested for a time in one of the houses on the front. It had rained most of the day, and by now we were soaked to the skin. My army boots and feet were saturated, so I found a pair of sandals which were several sizes too small. I cut out the toes, abandoned my boots and socks and was then much more comfortable. Early in the evening we went down to the beach, where we found thousands of other troops from every type of regiment in rough queues about six deep stretching down from the sand dunes to the water's edge. We could see the outline of Dunkirk a few miles to the west on our left. The town and the mole, still little damaged, were mostly hidden by black smoke, punctuated by the flashes of bombs as the Germans desperately tried to destroy it. As there seemed to be no movement in the queues and no evidence of evacuation from the beaches, we decided to stay in the dunes where we rested until about 2 a.m. Some years after the war when Sheila and I were on a motoring holiday in northern Europe we made a detour and visited Bray Dunes. It was still recognisable, but how different - it is now a small very picturesque seaside resort again. The main difference was several hideous concrete bunkers erected later in the war by the Germans against the invasion by the Allied Forces.

May 29ᵗʰ - Wednesday

The rain of the previous day had given way to a bright sunny morning, which developed into a lovely warm Spring day. As there was still no movement in any of the queues we spent a few hours in 'our house' - Tom Whitby, ever the gentleman, took off his boots before climbing on to an expensive eiderdown in one of the bedrooms, not realising that in a matter of hours it would be in the hands of the Germans. About 7 in the morning we returned to the beach. There was much air activity and a destroyer racing up and down the coast was sunk by bombs, as was a Red Cross hospital ship moored about half a mile offshore. There were many bombing raids on the troops on the beach during the day. Whenever planes appeared the troops would scatter and take what cover there was among the dunes. Fortunately the bombs were all of small anti-personnel type and, exploding in the soft sand, caused very few casualties. Once the planes had gone, the queues quickly reformed. During the late afternoon the word was passed round that our CO, who was still with us, had volunteered the remains of HQ platoon to act as stretcher bearers and helpers to a group of wounded men who had been given priority and were down at the water's edge. In the early evening we were told to go down to the sea, where we found a medium-sized rowing boat with a set of oars. We assisted some of the wounded on board and as I had done a bit of 'holiday rowing', I took over the oars. I suppose there were about half a dozen wounded and perhaps the same number of our lads - it certainly seemed a heavy load as I pulled away from the shore. Fortunately the sea was very calm and there were no planes about. Our destination was a small cargo boat moored about half a mile from the shore, and I suppose it took about half an hour to reach it. On arrival the crew quickly hauled the men on board and I found myself alone, still at the oars, and I realised that I would have to return to the beach for another load - this time, with an empty boat, the going was much easier. On arrival at the beach I took on another batch of walking wounded and a few more from 3 TCC. Again it was an uneventful trip back to the boat, which was Greek and called the *Patria*. History repeated itself and once again I found myself rowing alone for the shore. Again I took another batch and this time I decided that 'enough was enough', so when we reached the

Patria I made sure that I was one of those who scrambled aboard. I have no idea who, if anyone, took over 'my' boat. By now it was late evening and on deck I sat down in a corner and promptly fell fast asleep. I have no idea what time the *Patria* left the beach, but it must have been some time during the night. Again we were lucky and the crossing was uneventful.

May 30th - Thursday

I was woken by a shout that land was in sight and we docked at Margate some time in the morning. There was a small crowd of subdued people as we marched ashore and a few women made sympathetic comments about my toe-less sandals (What a contrast to the tumultuous reception we had received when we drove into Brussels a few days ago). After collecting tea and sandwiches from the WVS we were marched to the station, where we boarded a special troop train. It left with little delay and we arrived at our destination, Rhyl, in the late evening.

May 31st - Friday

At the reception barracks some time after midnight there was minimum formality. After giving our names and unit we were issued with a knife, fork and spoon, two blankets, given a huge meal and taken to dormitories where we were allowed to sleep for as long as we liked. We eventually woke in the middle of the morning and, after a good breakfast, were free for the rest of the day.

June 1st - Saturday

Jack and I wandered about the camp, had haircuts and shaves and after the evening meal, went to the cinema in Rhyl. Naturally at this time leave was uppermost in all our thoughts, but it was to be a fortnight before 'they' would let us go.

In retrospect this was probably right - the psychological impact of releasing thousands of troops in our condition into the civilian population would have had a catastrophic effect on civilian morale: so we had to wait till we were fully re-kitted out and made to look something like the real soldiers we were supposed to be, instead of the rabble that had left the beaches of Dunkirk.

PREFACE

I feel I must commence this, the second chapter of my war time story, with an apology. Whereas the first part dealt almost exclusively with the military campaign in France and Belgium, this part deals more with 'affairs of the heart'. I have tried to restrict this aspect as much as possible, but, apart from a few incidents, our military function during these two and a half years varied very little and became more or less routine. However the third and final chapter will revert to more military action and the romantic aspect will be non-existent.

1996

CHAPTER 2

ENGLISH INTERLUDE
June 1940 to April 1943

Following our evacuation from Dunkirk, we stayed at Rhyl for a week and, during this time, there were no parades or drills of any sort, just plenty of good food and sleep, and slowly the nightmare that was spawned on the beaches of Dunkirk gradually faded into the background of our minds. During this period we were fitted out with new uniforms and equipment. After a week, on Friday June 7th we were moved to Cleve Prior, a village in the Cotswolds, and on Sunday June 9th I hitch-hiked with Wilf Smith, one of the lads from Workshops and who had travelled with me from Birmingham, for an unofficial weekend at home. On Monday June 10th I arrived back at Cleve Prior to find the unit, with all my kit, had left. I traced it to the aerodrome at Witney in Oxfordshire and obtained a lift there in a lorry. Here we met up with the remains of 3 Troop Carrying Company and found that most of our 'gang' had survived and there were many happy reunions.

At this point the title of the unit was changed. It appears that, although the troop carrying companies had more than fulfilled their purpose in France and Belgium, this specific use was now over and we were renamed 72 General Transport Company. The only big change was that a fourth platoon 'D' was added, thus increasing our carrying capacity by a third. On June 15th we were all granted the long awaited 5 days leave and Jack and I travelled by truck to Oxford, where I caught a train to Birmingham and Jack went on to Wigan. We returned to camp on the 20th and on the 24th by some oversight on my part, I found myself transferred to 'B' platoon as a driver and so no longer 'regimentally employed'. I reluctantly moved out of HQ hut and into a tent and for the next four weeks had to endure the rigours of platoon life, including 24-hour guard duty in the guardroom at the entrance to the camp.

Here I must relate my one and only contact with what was the scourge of troops in World War One - Lice - It happened like this. When on guardroom duties one had to spend 24 hours in the confines of the guardroom, doing two hours on duty and four off. During the night we were allowed to sleep, fully dressed apart from boots in case the guard had to be 'turned out' for any reason. At that time there were communal blankets in the guardroom bunks, so it only needed one infected soldier to sleep in them and anyone following also became infected. I managed to get rid of them, but it was a very unpleasant experience. Later on, when things were more settled, we each had our own blankets and whenever we were required to do any night duty away from our own billet, we took our blankets with us.

We were paraded at 8.30 each morning and told which duties we would be allocated for the following twenty four hours. These were varied, road patrol along the aerodrome perimeter, road blocks, fire picquet, mobile patrol or stand-by. Guards and patrols were mounted at 3 p.m. each day and lasted twenty-four hours, after which we were free for the rest of that day. This routine lasted until the middle of July, when I 'wangled' a few days break. It happened like this. Ever since early childhood I had a badly deformed septum in my nose and now thought that, although it caused me no inconvenience, I might get it seen to by the army. I therefore reported sick to the M.O. at Witney, thus escaping one day's guard duty. He decided to refer me to a higher-up M.O. at Stow-on-the-Wold, whom I saw the next day, another day's freedom. He in turn referred me to an ear, nose and throat specialist at 35 General Hospital in Oxford, where I attended the following day. By now I was dealing with the 'top brass' in the Royal Army Medical Corps who was charming, but informed me firmly that, in his opinion, there was no urgency about my condition, a diagnosis I could have told him myself. After leaving the hospital I had a meal and went to the cinema and then caught a train back to camp. This little exercise had given me three days quite legitimate freedom from all duties.

On July 24th I managed to get myself transferred back to HQ Platoon as a Motor Cyclist again, thus leaving all guard duties (and lice) behind. The next day, Thursday July 25th we all moved to Adderbury, a small village just south of Banbury; our HQ was installed in Adderbury House, a small stately home requisitioned by the army, like so many at that time. The old Orderly Room staff found a vacant room at the top where we settled ourselves. There was little of interest to report during the next four weeks. As HQ Motor Cyclist I travelled all round the Cotswolds, enjoying the beautiful scenery in mostly fine weather. There was a Services Canteen in the village and we went to innumerable films in Banbury and elsewhere. This placid routine continued until August 23rd, when I qualified for a further 7 days leave. I hired a taxi to Banbury station, where I caught a train to Birmingham and so home. My sister had got my old Morris Eight going, so I was able to get about, though petrol was scarce. The days were spent playing tennis, visiting old friends and generally becoming a civilian again for a few all too short days. Night bombing had started and, as we lived in an old two-storied house, we spent the nights in the cellar which my father had had reinforced. On Monday night there was a very bad raid and we spent several hours dealing with many incendiaries that had fallen all around. From our high position to the south of Birmingham we could see fires blazing all over the city. After the 'all-clear' we eventually bedded down in the lounge about 4 a.m. The next day many roads in our locality were closed owing to delayed-action bombs. On the 29th I said my goodbyes, caught a train to Banbury, and then a bus back to Adderbury House. It seemed a strange incongruity that, down in the comparative peace and quiet of the Oxfordshire countryside, the army 'on active service' should be having such a peaceful time, while civilians only a few miles to the north were living in constant noise, action and real danger. But that is the way of modern warfare.

The next day, August 30th, I resumed my normal motor cycling duties - there was a rumour of an invasion in Kent, and in the middle of the night we were all turned out and took up defensive positions round the house, but it proved to be unfounded.

This routine continued for the ensuing week, until on the 9th September there was talk of a move to Essex, but this was later amended to Kent. Before we left we were told the reason for our move. The Germans had launched heavy bombing raids on London and Air Force bases in the south-east, preparatory to an invasion. This could not take place until the RAF had been eliminated and the Germans had full control of the skies. Thus the whole of the south-east of the country had become one vast defensive zone, with many ammunition dumps and anti-aircraft batteries and searchlights. All the dumps had to be constantly replenished and the main job of our unit was to ferry the shells etc. from the railheads to the various dumps.

On the next day the move took place and we travelled in a large convoy to our new location, Westerham on the Kent/Surrey border, a move that was to have a profound effect on the lives of both Jack and myself. We arrived late at night amid bombs, guns and searchlights. We bedded down in the back of a lorry and awoke next morning very cold and stiff and borrowed a bucket of hot water from a cottage for a wash and shave before moving into our new billets. The platoons were housed in large requisitioned country houses with their vehicles hidden in neighbouring woods and lanes. 'A' platoon was on Farley Common just above Westerham; 'C' platoon was a few miles away at Crockham Hill, while 'B' and 'D' platoons were detached to another command. Workshops was in a requisitioned garage at Brasted, a few miles to the east on the road to Sevenoaks. HQ platoon was in a house called 'The Pheasantry' overlooking the village green in the centre of Westerham, and the Orderly Room and Officers Mess were in a lovely old house called Squerreys Court, now a National Trust property, just outside the village, with the Sergeants' Mess in a smaller house a few miles up the road. The owner of Squerreys still resided in one half of the house and the Officers Mess had the other, with the Orderly Room occupying a large hall on the first floor overlooking the extensive grounds, a truly idyllic spot.

I was on duty the next day and during the morning there were four air raid alerts with many flights of German bombers escorted by fighters heading north. After midday I was sent on a detail, during which I saw many more planes - this was to become a regular sight during the ensuing months. This area where we were now stationed became known as 'Bomb Alley' because of the many bombs that fell there, some aimed at Biggin Hill, a famous fighter base a few miles to the north, but many more were jettisoned when the bombers failed to penetrate the anti-aircraft guns and the balloon barrage of the London defences. Another possible target was Chartwell, Churchill's country house only a mile or so to the south. He visited it whenever he could manage a few hours respite and we usually knew because of the heightened security. There was a Canadian unit concealed on the roads round Chartwell and anyone passing that way was liable to be challenged.

Members of HQ Platoon on the village green, Westerham.
Author - back row, second from left, Jack - back row, third from right.

I got back to HQ about 4 o'clock and settled in the Orderly Room with Jack, who was on night duty. Our new facilities were very different to those at Authieulle - for a start we had electric light, (when it was not cut off by enemy action) and telephones. The main difference was that only the duty clerk and Motor Cyclist slept there. The rest of the O.R. staff had to eat and sleep at the 'Pheasantry' in the village, about ten minutes walk away. Not nearly as cosy as our French cottage.

On Wednesday, Sept. 18th, one incident occurred that caused much amusement. I was returning from a long detail to Tunbridge

Wells when, just outside Southborough, I was passed by a small pick-up - the dreaded Military Police. It signalled me to stop and a very irate officer got out and strode up to me saying I had been speeding and 'we had the devil of a job catching you' - he was followed by his corporal and returned to his pick-up, leaving the NCO to record my offence. I produced my AB 64 (a soldier's pay book and identity document carried at all times) and my work ticket, for once all in order. He took down the details in his note-book and returned my AB 64 saying I should report the incident to my officer and a report would follow. When he handed me back my pay book I noticed that there was something in it that wasn't mine, but I accepted it with an apology and we parted, he to his van, which turned round and headed back towards Tunbridge Wells and I mounted my bike and continued back towards Westerham. When I considered I was well out of their area I stopped and looked in my pay book, to find the corporal had left his notebook in it. I was naturally cock-a-hoop - I had scored off the hated 'Red Caps', as it was impossible that he would remember my name and unit. On my return I reported the incident to the Adjutant, omitting the notebook part - he was not at all concerned, merely saying that he could do nothing until he received the report from the CMP, but that I should warn other drivers of the speed trap. Naturally we heard no more about it. An added bonus, if that's the word, was that in addition to my entry, there were details of all the other unfortunates who had been stopped for various offences that day, all of whom would wonder why they never heard any more about their misdemeanours. I still have that notebook among my wartime souvenirs.

And now I must digress and tell a little of our spare-time ac-tivities during these days at Westerham. There was the usual village hall in the centre of the village and Pitt's Cottage, which I must describe at some length, as it figured so largely in our lives. It was a 13th Century house, but much bigger than a cottage. It was so called because William Pitt the Younger, British Prime Minister from 1783, used it as his hunting lodge when he was in the county. At some time before the war it had been converted into a very good-class restaurant, serving coffee, luncheons and teas. At the outbreak of war it was owned and run by a Miss Wilson, a charming old lady, and staffed by a number of girls and ladies from the village, and a few who lived in. About this time a regiment of Canadians was billeted near Westerham, who, according to the local police, were not used to our strong English beer, and were 'making a bit of a nuisance' of themselves. The police asked Miss Wilson if she would consider opening her tea-room as a canteen in the evenings, in the hope that the Canadians would forsake their beer for something less potent. Miss Wilson, being a very patriotic old lady, readily agreed and arranged with her resident staff that they would serve in the canteen after the restaurant had closed. Of course the Canadians were not in the least interested in coffee and tea, but to the local English soldiery it was like home from home, somewhere warm and comfortable where they could relax, write and read letters, talk and enjoy snacks at very reasonable prices. This was the position on our arrival in Westerham and Pitt's Cottage soon became our regular haunt, especially for the orderly room staff. It was situated half way between Squerreys and the Pheasantry so we had to pass it on our way to and fro. Here I should mention that transport was much 'tighter' than in France. We could no longer 'lay on' a truck unofficially, as every detail had to have a work ticket signed by an officer, so we had to walk or catch buses.

Pitts Cottage, Westerham, Kent.

And now I must tell you about the four staff who 'lived in' at Pitts and who were to figure so largely in our lives. First there was Sheila, a stunning redhead of 26. She had been employed by Miss Wilson as a cake maker, but found the early rising (5 a.m.) and the hard work hand-mixing (no electric blenders at Pitts in those days) too exhausting, so asked to be transferred to the tea-room. Her parents were separated, her father a practising doctor in Luton and her mother living in a hotel in Penzance. She also had a married sister with a small son, whose husband had been invalided out of the RAF, also living just outside Penzance. Sheila's great friend was Marjorie, a few years older, who was later to marry the RASC Captain in charge of the RASC supply depot where I later collected the unit's rations. The other two were Hope and Eve, who were later to join the WRNS (Womens Royal Naval Service). These four were great friends and slept in two rooms at the top of Pitts among the cornflakes and mice, when it was quiet. But on most nights when bombing was severe they retreated to the cellar and slept among the coal. Miss Wilson, or Auntie Elsie as she became know to us, had an office-cum-bed-room on the first floor to which she retired when the restaurant closed, and we saw little of her during the evenings. She also owned a guest house just across the road from Pitts, appropriately called 'Over-the-Way', and a book shop a few yards up the road where teas were also served. Later on this had a direct hit from a small bomb, but fortunately, no one was hurt.

On the night of September 19th a message had to be taken to HQ Eastern Command at Hounslow. Fortunately for me the duty officer said it could wait until the morning, so I set off at 6 a.m. It had been a bad night and I went through Croydon, Purley, Mitcham and Kingston and was appalled at the amount of bomb damage everywhere, especially the result of a parachute mine that had got entangled in a tree and caused terrible havoc. I was very thankful that my trip had been deferred. The rescue services were still searching the ruins for any possible survivors. I was back about 11 a.m. - it had rained hard all morning and I was very wet. That night I had to take messages to all platoons in pitch dark, a nightmare ride, but luckily only local.

On some mornings when I was not pushed for time I would call at Pitts, seat myself among the local gentry and ask for coffee

Sheila

and Welsh Rarebit, one of my weaknesses. It was not until much later that Sheila told me the consternation this had caused. While all the others were rushing around with coffee and biscuits, some-one, usually Sheila, had to drop everything to make my Welsh Rarebit. I must say I was never refused.

Auntie Elsie, Sheila and Pam outside Pitt's.

There was a small cinema in Westerham, but we usually pre-ferred to catch a bus to Sevenoaks, which had a much better one adjacent to the bus station. On Sunday, September 29th the Quar-termaster asked me if I would like to become the company Storeman. With winter coming on and all the hazards of motor cycling in such conditions, it didn't take me long to accept. So I gave up the bike the next day and once again joined the orderly room staff, but this time as 'Q' Storeman. So from this time my daily routine was quite changed as follows. A three-tonner was detailed for 'rations' and reported to me at Squerreys about 9 each morning. We then went to the local RASC Supply Depot just a few miles up the road to collect all the rations for the whole unit. These were mostly tinned or packets, but included fresh bread, meat and vegetables. The meat was drawn in huge quar-ters. We then returned to Squerreys. My 'Store' was a large circular dairy set just behind the house with a stone shelf all round the inside. All the rations were unloaded, and, while our butcher cut up the meat into family-sized joints, I split the rations up into six separate lots, the two largest for the two platoons (the other two were still on detachment), two smaller ones for Workshops and HQ platoon, and two even smaller ones for the officers' and sergeants' messes. This usually took us up to lunchtime when we broke off and went up to the Pheasantry for our midday meal. On our return the six lots of rations were again loaded onto the truck and we went round delivering them to the various cookhouses. We usually got back about 4 o'clock, when the lorry was dismissed and I went to the orderly room to fill in returns, collect details of numbers for whom rations were to be drawn the next day etc. etc. Work in the orderly room usually finished about 5 o'clock when we all, except for the duty clerk and duty motor cyclist, returned to our billet for our evening meal and to get ready for whatever we had planned for the evening.

Barbara, Hope, Sheila and Marjorie outside Pitt's.

Ever since my early visits to Pitts I had taken a fancy to Sheila and one day in early October I plucked up courage and asked her if she would go to the pictures with me. Her reply was that she would, but only on condition that Jack and I made up a foursome with her and a friend. To this we readily agreed, and, after some thought, Sheila decided that Hope would be the most compatible companion for Jack, so it was agreed that the four of us would go to the film at Sevenoaks the following Friday. Jack and I both hurried through our duties that afternoon and called for the girls at 5.30. We caught the bus to Sevenoaks and saw 'Night Train to Munich'. Afterwards we had coffee and sandwiches at the cinema restaurant and then caught a bus back to Westerham. It was a very happy evening, the first of many, and Sheila soon gave up her 'foursome' condition.

On October 29th I had some very disturbing news from home. Our house had been very badly damaged by a large bomb that had exploded at the bottom of the garden. The whole of the rear of the house was wrecked, but the front was still habitable. Fortunately no one was hurt, as all were in the cellar at the time. I thought of asking for compassionate leave, realised that there would be little I could do, so decided to wait until my next leave.

Birmingham home damaged by bomb.

The platoons soon settled down in their respective houses, though in fact they were out on detail most of the time with haversack rations for their midday meal and the proper meal on their return. In addition to the sleeping quarters, there was a mess room where they had their meals and a large room for recreation. As they became established, the 'Q' corporal in the platoons put orders in to Pitts for trays of rock cakes and doughnuts, which they collected and sold for a small profit that went towards mess funds.

One day our 'gang' all bought Lyons Fruit Tarts in cartons from a shop in the village. In the evening at Pitts we all produced them and asked for plates and knives! The response from the girls was unprintable, but they soon appreciated the joke.

One evening during one of the usual raids one bomb fell unpleasantly close to Pitts - we were all in the tea-room at the time and the four girls happened to be in the kitchen. Sheila asked Hope to go and see what we were doing. She poked her head round the tea-room door and reported back that we were all sitting round as if nothing had happened, so they were reassured. When Sheila told me about this later, I said that if Hope had looked in a couple of minutes earlier, she would have found us all underneath the tables.

And so November and December passed very pleasantly and my relationship with Sheila slowly developed from 'dates' into something deeper. Because we had both had disastrous engagements just before the war, we were both very hesitant about committing ourselves and we discussed our feelings for each other endlessly without coming to any definite conclusion. We saw each other most nights and went to the occasional dance with Jack and Hope, whose romance seemed to be growing in parallel with ours. One incident caused the four of us a lot of anger and frustration. We had seen a dance advertised just outside Sevenoaks and decided we would like to go. We hired a taxi, but on arrival found it was 'Officers Only' and we were turned away. You can imagine our feelings. 'Courting' (that good old-fashioned word) under these conditions was fraught with difficulty: the 'black-out', cold and wet winter evenings, bombs, guns and searchlights every night, and my anxiety about my family at home etc. etc.

On December 7th I heard from home that my grandma had

passed away. Grandpa had died a few years earlier before the war in 1937 and for the last few months she had been living with my parents in Birmingham. She was 87, so had lived to a good age, but it was cruel that the last year of her long life should be spent under such severe wartime conditions. I could not get home for her funeral, but 'Quarter' promised that I would get Christmas leave, so I had to be content with that.

My 7 day leave commenced on Dec. 23rd and when I got home I found the house in a dreadful mess, even worse than I had imagined. It was now quite uninhabitable, but luckily my father had managed to rent a big house at Knowle, a small village about ten miles from Birmingham and so well away from the persistent bombing. The first thing I had to do when I got home was to get my old Morris Eight going again. A friend took the battery away for charging and, after a struggle, I got it working. Most of my leave was spent ferrying our personal belongings from the old house to the new one; on several occasions we found things that had been packed up ready to move the next day, had been looted overnight. Father and mother looked very tired and I applied, unsuccessfully, for an extension of leave, but in reality had no grounds. During this all too brief break I was able to visit several friends and help the family settle in their new home. In the evenings we played bridge and board games, but my heart was not really in any of it and I kept thinking about Sheila and wondering what she would be doing. I think this leave probably made me realise how much Sheila had come to mean to me, and finally acknowledge that I had fallen in love with her. Towards the end of my leave I phoned the Adjutant but had no luck with the extension of leave; so on Friday December 27th, I was seen off by the family from Snow Hill Station and arrived back at Westerham about 6.30. After reporting back I went down to Pitts but it was very crowded so Sheila and I had no chance to talk. The warning went about 10.30 so I returned to the orderly room. I had a brief chat with Sheila on the phone before turning in. I was on O.R. duty on New Year's Eve and heard the celebrations on the radio and wondered what the New Year would hold for me.

1941

The old routine of rations and visits to the cinema was resumed, but in addition, when we felt extravagant, Sheila and I would sit in the lounge of the Amhurst Arms, a very decent pub at Riverhead just outside Sevenoaks, and drink sherries, but we couldn't afford this very often.

One momentous event happened to me on January 7th - I had long been promised promotion, and on this day it actually happened and the announcement in Part II orders for that day read: 'T/117503 Driver A.O. Bennion is promoted to Local Acting Unpaid Lance Corporal w.e.f. 7/1/41' - the longest title for the lowest rank NCO in the army. So I spent a pleasant half hour sewing on my new stripes. But it was not to last long. There was a guardroom situated in a lodge at one of the entrances to Squerreys, manned twenty-four hours by a corporal and eight men. I was on orderly room duty on the night of Jan. 9th, and was about to turn in around midnight, when the guard corporal arrived to say that a prisoner had escaped from the guardroom by climbing out of a window. I said I would report it and he left. I got out the necessary form and began to type out the report, when there was a loud hammering on the wall and the C.O., whose bedroom was next to the orderly room, shouted at me to stop typing and go to bed. So I did. I finished the report as soon as I got up next morning and handed it to the Orderly Officer when he arrived at about 9. The next thing I knew was that I was up on a charge of 'Failing to report the escape of a prisoner to an officer', marched in front of the C.O., and, in spite of my protests, I was found guilty and 'reduced to the ranks'. Everyone from the CSM down was most sympathetic and felt I had been treated most unfairly. However, 'c'est la guerre', but I probably created a record in holding a promotion for the shortest time in the army. This also happened to be my 25th birthday - what a way to celebrate!

Talk between Sheila and myself about our future continued, still with no satisfactory conclusion, but now we were discussing the possibility of marriage quite freely. On February 3rd I took the bull by the horns and asked Sheila if she would marry me. She said, 'Yes, I will marry you,' and so from then on our talk was not about future possibilities but definite plans for our future to-gether. We neither of us wanted to wait, for several reasons; firstly, the future was so uncertain - either of us could be killed by a stray bomb at any time; secondly, I had no idea how long our unit would continue to be in the Westerham area - we could receive a move-ment order at any time, and it would very likely be overseas. We had reached the obvious conclusion that, if we got married, we would have to continue as we were, i.e. I in the army and Sheila at Pitts. Sheila naturally wanted a church wedding and we made enquiries about a special licence, but the cost ruled this out. We enquired about a local church wedding but the matter of banns and other formalities meant further delays; so, reluctantly, we settled for a Registry Office ceremony that could be arranged at short notice and with minimum fuss.

Soon after all this, I went down with a mild attack of 'flu and our Medical Orderly gave me an 'Excused all Duties' and I moved my bed into his sick bay for a few days, followed by four days sick leave. I travelled up to Birmingham on February 13th and had a somewhat tense leave with the family. When I told them of our wedding plans they were shocked, to put it mildly, and I suppose naturally jumped to the conclusion that we were 'having' to get married. Nothing was said to this effect, but I guessed that this was what they were thinking. Only Sheila and I knew that this was a physical impossibility. They could not understand why we were in such a hurry - both my father and mother were regular churchgoers and at that time a registry office wedding was just 'not done'. So altogether I was not sorry when the four days came to an end and I could return to Westerham and Sheila. We contacted the Registry Office at Sevenoaks and arranged for the wedding on Saturday March 1st. During the preceding week I rang round to several hotels, mainly in the Cotswold area to try to book a room for our honeymoon, but all were full, so I had to leave it to Sheila. She, Auntie Elsie and Marjorie went up to London to do some shopping and called at Selfridge's Travel Dept. They said that they would definitely book us in somewhere and that we should call in after the ceremony to find out where. So I suppose we must have been one of very few couples who, at the marriage ceremony, had no idea where they were going to spend their wedding night.

The whole thing had to be kept a close secret; Jack and I were neither of us drinkers and we knew that if the lads got to know about it there would be a 'stag night' with all sorts of high jinks, which was the last thing I wanted. So only two other people knew. The Adjutant, who had to sign my leave pass and Johnnie Bewg, an awfully nice lad whom we knew we could trust. And so, after all our agonising, our wedding day dawned. I can do no better than to quote Jack's diary entry for that day. He sent Sheila and me a copy when he and Hope sent us an anniversary card for our 55th Anniversary this year.

Extract from Jack's 1940 - 41 War Diary, Page 74

Arthur managed to get his leave from March 1st and the wedding was fixed for that day - Saturday. As everything was more or less secret, it was necessary to tell a few 'white lies' to inquisitive people. The arrangements were as follows - Sheila, Miss Wilson, Hope and Marjorie from Pitts would proceed to the Registry Office in Sevenoaks by taxi and Arthur and I were to go on the 9.45 a.m. bus from Westerham to Sevenoaks. At 10.15 a.m. Arthur and Sheila were married, Miss Wilson and myself being witnesses. From the Registry Office we went to Hope's home where Mrs Wickenden had wedding cake and sherry ready. Mr and Mrs Bennion stayed for a very short time and rushed off and caught the 11.04 a.m. to London. Difficulty had been experienced in obtaining accommodation, but this was settled at the last moment. Then Miss Wilson, Hope and Marjorie (and self) returned to Westerham on the 11.15 bus. Back to the office, and what a stir the wedding caused. Better left to the imagination. Next evening Hope and I went to Botley Hill Farm, walking half the way back. Thus four of us started off - Sheila, Hope, Arthur and self. Now only the two of us are left single. It will be very strange now that Arthur is married, because we have been together since embarking for France in

1939 and have seen a lot together. Anyway, I think they will be very happy. I hope so.

This was the end of Jack's diary entry, but in his letter that accompanied it he wrote - 'My prediction at the end of the extract was pretty accurate, wasn't it?' - how right he was.

But back to March 1st. When Sheila and I arrived in London we went straight to Selfridges to find out what they had been able to fix up for us. They had done us proud, and we found we were booked in to the Spa Hotel at Tunbridge Wells in Kent. We had a meal in London, went to a News Theatre and then caught a train for Tunbridge Wells, passing through Sevenoaks on the way. The hotel was magnificent, a big four-star edifice, mainly occupied by high-ranking officers who didn't expect to be sharing their dining room with a lowly 'other rank'. I have a feeling that the staff knew or guessed that we were on our honeymoon and were very kind and the service was excellent. We spent a very happy four days there walking round and shopping. On the Thursday we left and went back to London to catch a train for Birmingham, where I had promised that Sheila should meet my family. It was a very strained meeting, as one would expect, but all went off quite well - in addition to meeting my father and mother, there was my sister Margaret and two aunts, so poor Sheila was indeed 'thrown in at the deep end'. She coped well, but it was a relief when we said goodbye the next morning to return to London and Westerham. Sheila had promised Auntie Elsie that she would be back on Saturday to help with a big wedding reception for which she was catering. During the reception the bride's father announced that one of the 'waitresses' had cut short her own honeymoon in order to be there, so they toasted her in champagne. This was a typically kind gesture initiated by Auntie.

And so we reverted to our usual routines, except that now we were married we were much happier, with all our discussions and uncertainties behind us. I was able to apply for the occasional 'sleeping out' pass, and we found a small guest house in Westerham called Stakes House, where we could go. We also booked a room at the Amhurst Arms when we were feeling in an extravagant mood, but this was very pricey. Auntie was very kind, and let us use an upstairs tearoom at Pitts, which was not used in the evenings; so, when Sheila was off duty, we used to cook our suppers in the kitchen, take it upstairs and eat it in front of the fire, and it was all very cosy.

All went on very happily until the inevitable blow fell and we learnt that the unit was moving out of Westerham and going to the Ascot area. It could have been worse; at least it was within a reasonable distance of Westerham and we were still on 'home service'. We moved out on May 21st and soon settled down in our new surroundings. Again all the platoons were billeted in large country mansions scattered around Ascot, Sunninghill, Sunningdale and Bracknell. One was even in one of the Administrative buildings on the racecourse itself. The orderly room staff (our gang) slept in the billiard room (complete with full-sized table) on the top floor of one mansion, with the officers' mess below. My ration store was a tin hut in the grounds of 'C' platoon's billet, called Birchcommon, and the mess room was in a large marquee erected in the grounds next to the cookhouse. A certain Lady Webb had opened part of her house as a canteen, where we could get tea, coffee and cakes, and read and write. I'm not sure who she was, but she made us very welcome. She also had a tennis court which we were allowed to use. But of course for me the only thing I really wanted was to be able to get back to Westerham and Sheila as often as possible. Buses and trains were out, far too time-consuming and expensive, so I managed to find and buy a very old two-stroke motor-cycle. It let me down innumerable times, but somehow I always managed to get it going again, so the link with Pitts was restored. Petrol was quite a problem. Supplies to non-military vehicles was strictly controlled and rationed, but I overcame this problem in my own devious way. As I said, we were sleeping on the top floor of the officers' mess and after we turned in I used to stay awake, and, when I thought everyone was asleep, I crept down to the courtyard where the staff cars were parked and siphoned petrol from one of the tanks into bottles, which I hid in an outhouse. Luckily I was never caught, and so was able to make my trips to Westerham whenever I could get a pass. On several trips Jack came with me, riding pillion, but this extra load pushed up the petrol consumption, and we ran out on more than one occasion, but somehow I always managed to scrounge some from somewhere.

And so it was not an unpleasant summer- in addition to snooker on our own table, Lady Webb's canteen and tennis, there was a golf course on which we were allowed to play, with a set of clubs borrowed from the clubhouse, and an open-air lido called the Pantiles where we could swim.

About mid-June Sheila found she was pregnant - we were not surprised, as we had done nothing to avoid such an eventuality. We had realised that setting up home was quite out of the question under our present circumstances, but knew that, if a baby did materialise, she had two places where she could go. Her sister in Cornwall and my parents in Knowle. Sheila stayed on at Pitts till mid-August, when the work became too hard for her to continue. Rather against her own inclinations I persuaded her to move into a small hotel in Woking, a few miles from Ascot. She stayed there a week, and then moved to another one in Virginia Water, but it did not work out. I could not get to see her at all during the daytime, or even at nights when I was on duty. Consequently she felt very lonely after the communal life at Pitts and became very depressed. So at the end of August she moved up to Knowle and spent three weeks with my parents. In a way this was a relief - I had been continually trying to snatch a few precious hours with her, and feeling guilty when I couldn't, so now I was able to concentrate on my duties without any distractions. She then came back and we had two nights together at an hotel in Ascot before she returned to Cornwall in mid-October, this time to Looe, where her mother was now living in a hotel owned by friends.

In November I had seven days leave, the first two with Sheila at Penzance and the rest at Looe. The only item of interest at this time was that I got my stripes back, this time for a bit longer. I couldn't get Christmas leave, but was promised a pass for the New Year.

1942

It was only a 48-hour pass, which meant twenty-four hours travelling and only twenty-four hours with my wife, but we were able to see the New Year in together. This was to be my last leave before the birth of our baby, which we thought would be in mid-

February. On my return from leave I made myself popular with the lads by volunteering to do permanent night duty clerk in the orderly room. This was not out of any gesture of goodwill on my part, but simply so that I could be sure of getting the news from Cornwall without any delay when it came through. I had already 'laid on' a 48-hour pass immediately I had word, followed by a 7-day leave when Sheila and baby came out of the nursing home.

The phone message came on February 11th and I rushed down to greet the new arrival and to see if all was well. The 7 days leave was spent at Penzance - Eileen and family lived in a small house, so conditions were rather cramped, but we managed. Some time after that Sheila and Michael moved up to Knowle, where the new arrival was made a great fuss of, my parents' first grand-child. I had a further 7 days leave with them in May, and by now my parents had really taken Sheila to their hearts.

One of the perks of my job was that I was able to help in the food stakes whenever I went on leave. The army rations were more than plentiful, much better than the civilian ones, where even the most basic commodities were in very short supply and severely rationed. Whenever I went on leave I would take my respirator our of its haversack and hide it in my kitbag. The hav-ersack would then be filled with sugar, butter, bacon, cheese, etc. all of which were welcomed by my family, though with some qualms by my mother.

And so the summer passed with very little change in our cir-cumstances. Jack's romance with Hope was blossoming, and he visited Pitts whenever he could get the time off. Finally they got engaged and were married at Sevenoaks church on October 9th. I was best man and met his family who had come down from Southport for the occasion. Sheila and Michael were with my family at Knowle at the time, and Sheila left Michael with my mother for a few days, a charge she was only too happy to accept. At Sevenoaks we all had a grand reunion - the wedding reception was held at Aplins, a big restaurant in Sevenoaks, after which Jack and Hope left for London and their honeymoon, just as Sheila and I had done the previous year, only this time they knew where they were going. We all then returned to Pitts and after tea Sheila and I went to the Amhurst Arms for the night. Next day we went up to London, had a meal and saw a film. Sheila then returned to

Pitts and I to Ascot. We did the same again on the Sunday, after which I saw her off back to Knowle.

About this time my father bought another house in Birmingham, not far from the one that was wrecked. It had four bedrooms so they were quite able to accommodate their new family. They continued to live at Knowle until the new house was ready. I had another ten days leave in December and spent it at Penzance. Eileen had had another baby, a girl this time, born the previous July, so conditions in their small semi-detached house were even more cramped than before. On returning to the unit, I was detached to 'B' platoon as Q corporal at a place called Pratsham Grange for a week before returning to HQ with the C.O. a week before Christmas.

1943

During January and February I managed to get several weekend passes, spending them either in London with Sheila or at Knowle. In February Sheila and Michael went to stay with an old friend and her family at Chingford in Essex. On February 17th I got a 48-hour pass to spend with them there and on my return found I was once again in trouble. There had been a 'blitz' in my absence and, although I had a perfectly valid pass, I had failed to 'sign out', something that, although laid down, had never been insisted upon. So I was charged accordingly and once again 'reduced to the ranks', this time on a pure technicality. Considering the number of times I had taken time off without a pass at all, this was just bad luck. So the next weekend, in sheer defiance, I met Sheila, my parents and my sister Margaret in London, where we had dinner and I returned to Chingford with Sheila, where I spent the night, all without a pass. I returned to Ascot early the next morning with some apprehension, but all was well and I had got away with it. On many of these occasions Jack would 'cover' for me if he could. At the end of February Sheila and Michael moved back to Penzance.

About this time we were all engaged in a big exercise codenamed 'Spartan'. The whole unit was involved and it covered a large area of the south coast. In addition to my 'Q' duties I once again found myself on a bike, escorting convoys and doing the old traffic control routine. I have no idea of the purpose of this exercise but I covered over 600 miles during the fortnight the exercise lasted. Finally it ended on March 14th, and we returned to our base in Ascot.

Almost immediately on our return the dreaded 'top secret' movement order came through - our instructions to mobilise for overseas service. Pandemonium reigned. All passes were immediately cancelled and we began the involved process of sending everyone home on 10 days Embarkation Leave. This entailed an enormous amount of paperwork, leave passes, railway warrants, medical checks, innoculations, indents for new stores and equipment, new kit to be issued, etc. etc. At this time our destination was a closely guarded secret, the only clue was that we were issued with tropical uniforms.

My own leave was booked from March 18th to the 27th and we spend an idyllic 10 days in and around Penzance, only marred by the inevitable goodbye that loomed closer with every day that passed. Finally it arrived and Sheila and I had a tearful farewell on Penzance station. This was undoubtedly the saddest day of my life. We neither of us knew if or when we would ever see each other again. The fact that such partings were being enacted on countless stations all over the country by thousands of couples, as more and more troops were being sent overseas, was no consolation, and I can still see the pathetic figure of Sheila standing alone on the platform as the train slowly pulled away round the curve.

On my return I was once again plunged into the melee of mobilising - everything had to be completed by April 6th and in the intervening week all our vehicles were withdrawn apart from a few kept back for essential purposes. Sheila and I spoke on the phone every day, and we agreed that from that date we would number all our letters so that we would know if any had gone missing. I had so enjoyed the freedom and independence that my bike had given me that I again volunteered to be HQ Motor Cyclist and my application was accepted, so I drew all new M/C kit, including, this time, a revolver.

The one big disappointment was that Jack would not be going abroad with me. He had previously applied for a commission and had been accepted for training with several others. I had pondered long and hard about applying myself - the extra money (should I be successful) would be a great help, but it would mean leaving all the lads I had been with for so long. It was obvious that, once training was over, Jack and I would almost certainly be posted to different units among total strangers. Also I was not too keen on the rigid class system that still prevailed between the officers and other ranks. We got on extremely well with our officers, but the gulf was always there, and I could not forget the humiliation we four had felt at being turned away from the 'officers only' dance. So in the end I had decided to stay 'in the ranks', where at least I could remain among my friends. And so Jack and the others were excluded from the posting and would leave for their training unit when we left Ascot. So on April 1st Jack and I had a farewell meal together, followed by the inevitable film. Over the past few years we must have seen hundreds of films, averaging about three a week, first as a twosome, then a foursome and latterly again in pairs with Sheila and Hope. As Jack and I had shared so many experiences together, both military and personal, I feel I must sketch in what happened to him after he left Ascot.

He went first to a pre-OCU unit at Wrotham, followed by a three month course at Royal Engineer Field OCTU at Newark. After passing out, he was RTO (Rail Transport Officer) at Warrington for a time, whilst waiting to attend another course at Longmoor in Hampshire on the loading of troops and equipment in preparation for the 'D' day landings. From there he was posted to the Port of London and thence to Tilbury, where he was involved in the loading of 48 ships reinforcing the armies battling in Europe. After this he went across the Channel to Arromanches and thence to Dieppe, Ghent, Brussels, Hamburg, Kiel, Lubek and Antwerp. Jack finished his army career in Hamburg, after spending eighteen months in that 'battered but attractive city' - (his own words).

But back to Ascot. By April 6th all preparations for our departures were completed - our postal address was changed to APO 4605, which would give no clue as to our whereabouts, all ranks were 'confined to barracks' and all kit was packed. We were due to leave on the 9th. I was on duty in the office all the previous day and most of the night. I rang Sheila and we said our last goodbyes. I also rang my family. I was very sorry not to have been able to see them before we left, but they understood that my first priority was to my wife and son. I finally got to bed about 2 a.m. On Friday the 9th the whole company was paraded in the grounds of 'C' platoon and marched to Ascot station, where we boarded a troop train, and it was only then that we found that our immediate destination was Liverpool.

We arrived at Dockside Station and went straight aboard the *S.S. Franconia*, a troop ship of some 20,000 tons and capable of 15 - 20 knots. We learnt that there were over 4,000 troops on board. We spent the morning watching arrivals and departures and at about 6 o'clock the moorings were cast off and she moved to mid-river where she moored. Of course this was familiar ground to a lot of our territorial lads, whose homes were in the vicinity. I don't suppose our move from the dockside had anything to do with it, but it made any idea of a couple of extra days unofficial leave quite impossible. Conditions on board were cramped in the extreme. We slept in hammocks slung between pipes below decks. The noise of the plumbing made sleep very spasmodic, though the hammocks themselves were not too uncomfortable. On Sunday the 11th there was an inspection at 10 o'clock. We watched the last mail go ashore, together with some high-ranking officials and the ship fuel up. Boat drill was at 4.15 followed by some ack-ack practice. There was boat drill again the next morning and at 4.15 we weighed anchor and the *Franconia* left the Mersey. I stayed on deck till about 9 o'clock watching all the river traffic. On waking next morning we found we were in the mouth of the Clyde. We passed four aircraft carriers and six subs on our way up the river before mooring off Dunoon. At this time there was a medical inspection. The next day was wet and misty so boat drill was held inboard, and nothing much else happened, except that I developed a bad head cold. During the next day we watched fuel and water tankers alongside and the Commodore came on board and the ship was prepared for sailing. Merchant vessels were leaving all evening, but no sign of any movement by us. At 9.30 I went to bed, luckily my cold was much better. On Friday, the 16th, I woke to find us leaving the Clyde and heading north-west. The convoy consisted of about thirty ships, escorted by six destroyers and soon after these were joined by a Southampton class cruiser. On heading for the open sea, we saw the last of Scotland fall away astern as we turned due west.

The remainder of the voyage and where we were bound will all be revealed in Chapter 3.

PREFACE

O nce again I feel I must start Chapter 3 of my story with an apology. As I explained in the Preface to Chapter 1, the whole idea was started by my son, Michael, who was curious to learn about my wartime experiences. His whole life and career has always been associated with cars and motoring (he is with SAAB), which is why, in Chapter 1, I described our troop-carrying vehicles in such detail. In this chapter I drive an amphibious truck for seven months and I am afraid I have again been equally explicit in describing these very versatile and amazing vehicles. This is mainly for his benefit, and to other readers I offer this apology.

1996

CHAPTER 3

AFRICA - TUNISIA - SICILY - ITALY
April 1943 to December 1945

1943 in Convoy

Soon after leaving the Clyde estuary we were told that our destination was the port of Algiers on the North African coast. The voyage was fairly uneventful apart from a few scares and we continued to head west with the Irish coast invisible on our port bow. The convoy now consisted of about fifty ships, with an escort of one cruiser and seven destroyers, with a Sunderland flying boat keeping watch overhead. Boat drill was twice a day and we began our daily doses of anti-malaria tablets. At some stage we veered due south and on or about the 20th April we were off Cap St. Vincent and at this point were joined by a second cruiser. There was one submarine scare and the destroyers dropped several depth charges, but nothing materialised. About this time the convoy split in half, our half turning due east towards Gibraltar, while the other continued due south, presumably on its way to South Africa. We must have passed through the Straits during the night, as next morning found us sailing in the blue Mediterranean in bright sunshine. Of course during the whole voyage a strict black-out was observed, so it was strange that, on our first night in the Med., we saw a neutral cruise ship ablaze with lights.

Two natural phenomena impressed me during this phase of the voyage: firstly, shoals of porpoise or dolphins that raced ahead of the ship's bow wave, sometimes jumping right through it, and secondly, summer lightning - at night the whole horizon was a constant flicker of light but with not a sound - most uncanny.

We continued due east all that day with no land in sight, but the next morning found us quite close to the North African coast and we continued to hug the coastline until we reached Algiers - during the last few hours we had been escorted by three Spitfires, presumably from Malta, as we were now well within range of German bombers based in Sicily or southern Italy.

North Africa

We docked about midday on April 23rd in scorching heat and I was struck by the stately buildings and tropical vegetation. After some delay we marched ashore carrying rifle, small pack, steel helmet and one blanket. After a roll call, we marched about five miles to a rendezvous, where we were picked up by lorries and taken a further ten miles to a farm which was a reception area. The farm was wine-producing and after a make-shift meal we bedded down on the concrete floor of a barn - not the best night I have had.

Next day the unit began to settle in. The Orderly Room was set up in one of the rooms in the farmhouse, which was situated jut outside a village called BEN AIDA. Our vehicles and bikes had not yet arrived, so I was co-opted on to the orderly room staff to help with the paperwork that seemed to be never-ending, even when overseas. Our kitbags arrived on this day, and I was glad to unpack my 'Lilo' - this was my most valued possession, a single air mattress with a built-in pillow, and, when inflated, gave me a comfortable night's sleep, whatever the ground underneath. That evening a few of us walked into the village - we found no food, but bought a bottle of wine and a bag of dates, which we munched in the dusk on our way back to the farm. It was only next morning, when we looked at the remaining dates, in the bag, that we saw that they were riddled with maggots - ugh! I have never touched a date from that day to this. On this trip we also saw what appeared to be a large grasshopper, but which of course we later realised was a locust.

All our vehicles arrived a few days later, and I checked my new bike for any damage, but it appeared to be OK. At this time there was little motor cycle work, but, with George Sharp, the other

Maison Carrée

HQ motor cyclist, I managed a few practice runs in the surrounding country, very wild and awe-inspiring. On May 1st the title of our unit was changed yet again and we now became 72nd Amphibious Transport Company, the first of this type in the British Army. We were told that two platoons would continue to operate conventional land-based trucks, but the other two would be equipped with amphibious American trucks, which would arrive soon. For the next week there is little to report, the most exciting news was that we began to receive mail from home. We had more inoculations and visited a firing range for some rifle-firing practice, the first I have ever had after four years in the army. On May 9th the unit moved about 11 miles further east to another small town called MAISON CARREE, and we were issued with mosquito nets. On the 13th there was an air raid on Algiers, but we only heard it in the distance. We also had typhus inoculations. On the 16th I decided I would try to reach the Sahara Desert (!!!!), so set off on my bike on my own, (ostensibly on a training run). I headed south on a road that led into the heart of the Atlas Mountains, passing through several villages and climbing constantly. The surroundings got wilder and signs of human habitation less frequent. The scenery was superb, deep ravines, waterfalls, precipices, but the road was still quite good. Eventually I had to give up and turned round and retraced my steps. On checking on a map later I realised that I had barely penetrated the mountains at all, and that the desert was still a hundred miles or so beyond my turning point.

On May 22nd we moved yet again, this time still further east to a place called CAPE AOKAS. Myself and George were detailed to escort the CO's car and to do the usual traffic control. There was a mass of American military vehicles heading west returning from the front. We arrived about 7 in the evening and the orderly room was set up in a marquee on the top of a hill. At this time we were issued with two-man bivouacs, which would be our sleeping quarters for the next four weeks. These are small ridge tents, about six feet long, four feet wide and about three feet high, so they were really only suitable for sleeping. Their advantage was that each end was sealed with a mosquito net, so once inside there was no need for any other protection.

This location was very near the beach so we took every opportunity to swim and sunbathe - consequently several of us suffered horribly from sunburn, and I recall my shoulders blistered and I lost several layers of skin - entirely our own fault for not realising how strong the combination of Mediterranean sun and sea can be.

On May 24th several American Ducks arrived with their GI drivers and for several days they gave us demonstrations of how to drive through surf and driving on water. The name Duck is a synonym of the American manufacturers production code D.U.K.W. and the nickname was most apt. I was so intrigued by these novel vehicles that I felt I had to 'have' one - so once again I applied to be taken off the bike and transfer to a platoon where I would become a Duck driver. This was accepted and on the 26th I handed my bike and kit to Arthur Turner, who was to take my place as HQ motorcyclist.

A detail of drivers was sent off to collect our issue of Ducks while I and several others were detailed to drive heavy 5-ton vehicles to move RE stores from one depot to another. This only lasted a few days and when we returned to our base we found the Ducks had arrived, about 50 of them. Here I met and palled up with Jim Aspinall, a very quiet and studious lad from Leicester, who was to be my co-driver and we were to share many experiences together over the next six months. When we were allocated our own Duck (which I promptly christened *Maid of Penzance*) we immediately gave it a thorough check and found that the brakes were binding and the bilge pumps not working. The latter could wait, but the brakes had to be seen to at once. We worked on them and hoped we had cured the problem. On June 13th Duck Training began in earnest by a team of American GI instructors, this time on our own Ducks. Here I think I must digress and describe these versatile vehicles in some detail - (mainly for my son's benefit).

The Duck

The Duck is based on a standard GMC 3-ton truck with a six cylinder petrol engine with L/H drive. All six wheels are permanently driven through a manual 5-speed gearbox with an auxiliary low box giving ten gears in all. Built round this is a watertight hull and when afloat all wheels and axles are suspended in the

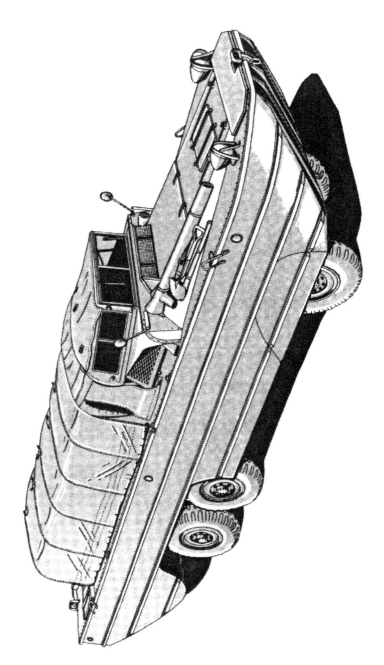

AMPHIBIAN TRUCK - THREE QUARTER FRONT VIEW

water. The tyres are a special feature, being wall-less with heavy duty tread and capable of being deflated to 8 p.s.i. When deflated the Duck is able to go over any soft ground or sand that a tracked vehicle can negotiate. There is a built-in compressor with a long rubber airline coiled behind the driver's seat. Later models were fitted with a built-in airline, through each wheel hub with six pressure gauges and valves on the dashboard enabling the driver to inflate or deflate the tyres without leaving his seat.

Driving technique on land was quite orthodox, apart from the size, 30 feet long by about 8 feet wide and capable of up to 70 m.p.h. However they were very sluggish on water, only being able to manage about 8 knots. On water it was driven by a propeller and rudder recessed in an arch under the stern of the hull, the rudder being operated by the steering wheel. The propeller was engaged by a single lever on the floor beside the driver. Driving on water one engaged the propeller and a low gear and set the hand throttle to maximum. As the pedals are not used when on water, a better view all round was obtained by driving standing on the back of the driver's seat (which hinged forward) and steering either by bending down or more usually with one foot on the wheel. There was a bilge pump driven by the engine for pumping water out of the bilges, but on our Duck it was a constant source of trouble and in spite of dismantling it several times, we could never be sure it would work - fortunately we never had to use it 'in anger'.

Other features, starting from the bow. Right at the front there was a hinged surfboard to protect the windscreen from damage when riding through heavy surf. Just behind this was a small watertight hatch giving access to the inside of the hull. Behind this was the main engine hatch, with a raised metal air intake grill at the rear. A large hand pump was strapped alongside this hatch, together with spades, picks and shovels. The driving cab was wide, with large exhausts on both sides through hooded metal grills. Between the driving cab and the main cargo hold was a narrow passageway extending the full width of the duck with a floor composed of three removable metal grills for access to the propeller shaft. It was also convenient as standing room for a few extra men if the hold was full. The cargo hold itself had eight stout removable wooden floor boards. As the main purpose of the Duck

AMPHIBIAN TRUCK - THREE QUARTER REAR VIEW

was loading cargo from over the side of ships, by means of derricks and cargo nets, the hold was always open, but they carried wooden hoops and a tarpaulin for use when the hold was used as a billet for the crew during maintenance.

On the rear deck, in addition to the spare wheel and anchor there was a rack for two cans of fuel and a small hatch for personal belongings. At the centre in the stern was the powered 'take off' (Americanism) or, as we would call it, a winch with 50 feet of steel cable. Beneath this was a stout tow hook. As there were no footholds on the outside of the hull and the top was about five feet high, scrambling aboard was a bit difficult, so we solved this little problem by making ourselves a short wooden ladder, which we carried behind the driver and this made life much easier.

Maintenance was of paramount importance - with all wheel and brake assemblies immersed in salt water most of the time, these had to be attended to regularly. After each spell of perhaps several weeks of continuous day and night working, a period of at least a week had to be set aside for maintenance. This was usually carried out by the crew in a field well away from the scene of operations, during which time we used the hold as our living quarters, eating and sleeping there. The two-man bivouac could be erected in the hold and with the tarpaulin erected for protection against the elements and an electric light rigged up from the battery, it was very comfortable. I didn't even have to blow up my Lilo by mouth. I just connected the Duck's airline to it, ran the engine for a few moments and it was fully inflated. In fact, it became a standing joke. In late evening when everyone was settling down for the night and a Duck engine would start up, someone would say, "There's Arthur blowing up his Lilo again." The cookhouse was usually sited in one corner of the field and we collected our food and took it back to the Duck. Of course on these occasions we were usually sited miles from anywhere, and even if there had been, we had no means of getting there, so we had to make our own amusements. Four of us got a bridge 'school' going and, with writing letters and reading, the time passed quite pleasantly.

Maintenance was concentrated on the wheels and brake assemblies - each one had to be stripped down to the last nut and bolt, even to replacing the rubber pistons in the master cylinders.

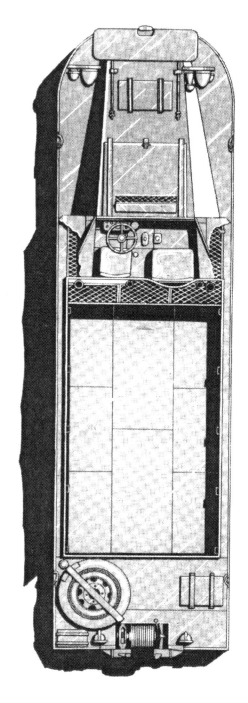

AMPHIBIAN TRUCK - TOP VIEW

Then cleaned in petrol, greased and re-assembled. The engine, largely protected from the salt water, only had the normal oil change and clean-up - anything more than this was done by a fully equipped American workshop nearby and any problems such as seized wheel nuts, spares and replacements. Also the whole of the outside of the hull had to be repainted frequently. All the above was learnt during our training sessions while still on the North African coast, so let us return there.

Concentrated training with the Ducks continued, interspersed with lectures on combined operations, servicing and sand driving, winching, etc. At this point we had a new C.O., a very welcome change, as our previous one had made himself very unpopular. The practical training on water was quite exciting - in addition to learning how to ride through surf and manoeuvre the unwieldy vehicles, we had to carry out various exercises in conjunction with an LST. The term is the abbreviation for Landing Ship Tank, but in fact they were much more versatile than that and transported every type of vehicle, including Ducks, guns and ambulances. They were a much smaller version of the modern roll-on, roll off ferry, with two decks and with room for just two lines of vehicles on each. They had two bow doors and a loading ramp raised and lowered by chains. As there is no room for turning or manoeuvring, all vehicles, when loading, had to be reversed on, ready for a quick drive off. They had a very shallow draught, enabling them to run right up to the beach and vehicles would then drive straight off on to the sand. They were very modern in design and built in large numbers in the States, even to having iced drinking water on tap. They carried basic anti-aircraft guns, but had to rely on escorts for any serious defence. Their total carrying capacity was 40 tanks, in four lines of ten, but this was greatly increased if smaller vehicles were carried.

Part of our training was with an LST moored off-shore. Its doors would be open and the ramp down in the water. We then had to try to board it from the sea. The theory was that you lined your Duck up in front of the ramp, engaged a low gear and charged like hell at the ramp - if you got it right, as soon as the front wheels hit the end of the ramp, they gripped and pulled the Duck forward until the rear wheels also gripped, when you had to slow down - fast! This was all right in theory, but the sea swell and movement of the ship made it very tricky, and many times we found ourselves trying to climb the ramp chains or missing the ramp altogether, when we would have to back off and start all over again. All great fun. Luckily we never had to do this exercise 'for real', but it all helped us to operate the Duck on water in difficult conditions. Needless to say, during most of this sea training we were soaked to the skin, but we wore very little and we soon dried off in the hot sun. In fact this period was more like a holiday camp than an army training exercise, and we were always ready to take to the water, day or night.

Two days into training I was detailed to take a naval officer and two ratings round to a neighbouring bay where they needed to take some soundings. This was my first trip on the Duck on my own, and all went well, but on returning to our own beach I found the brakes were still binding, so I handed it over to Jim to take to Workshops, while I used a practice Duck to take another naval officer and two more ratings round to another bay for a similar exercise. I recorded that on this day we had torrential rain, but it only lasted a short time and was a welcome change from the usual heat.

The Ducks head for the shore - by means of a simple lever power is switched from propeller to wheels.

A Duck manoeuvres alongside a ship - having picked up it's full load, it will be driven straight to the inland dump.

On June 19th after about a week of this intensive training, there were signs of a move and from now on I think it will be clearer if I revert to the diary format.

June 21st - Monday

Today we completed our Duck Training and were told to report to an RE Depot, where the Ducks were loaded with coils of Sommerfelt Tracking - this heavy duty wire mesh is laid down on beaches to enable wheeled vehicles to drive over soft sand. The two land-based platoons left, travelling east towards Tunisia and we are to follow later by sea on an LST.

June 24th - Thursday

We went in convoy to Bougie where we went aboard LST 320 - it left the docks at about 5.30 p.m. and joined a convoy of about 25 others. We bedded down on some packing cases in the hold.

June 25th - Friday

The convoy, escorted by several destroyers, headed due east, hugging the coastline. We happen to be the HQ ship with a Rear Admiral in charge of the convoy. There are 13 Ducks and one Jeep on the lower deck, but nothing on the upper one. Towards evening we are moored just off Bone, where we again slept in the hold.

TUNISIA

June 26th - Saturday

The convoy continues due east, passing Biserta about noon. Off Cap Bon at about 4 o'clock our convoy was attacked by a strong force of German bombers. The escorting destroyers responded and the attack continued for about an hour until three Spitfires appeared and the enemy planes withdrew. One destroyer dropped several depth charges and a large patch of blazing oil appeared over the spot, but we saw no sign of a submarine. There were no hits on the convoy, but one LST had to beach because its steering gear had been damaged. The air attack was resumed about 8 and went on intermittently until late evening. We eventually bedded down on the lower deck in our life jackets.

June 27th - Sunday

At about 9 o'clock we docked at SOUSSE and drove off the LST to an Assembly Area a short distance inland. There is much damage everywhere and at midday I was ordered to leave in convoy, leaving Jim behind. I drew petrol and rations and we left about 2 p.m. after we had been given routine landing instructions from a Capt. Masters. We arrived in another Assembly Area and parked in strict lines between olive groves according to our serial number. Each grove was labelled and the vehicles in that grove would constitute the cargo for one LST. The vehicles in our grove were an assorted lot, 3-tonners, ambulances, jeeps, personnel carriers and four Ducks. We were told that we were likely to leave tomorrow - we are part of Beach Group 20 and are attached to the 51st Highland Division, a crack unit in the British 8th Army.

June 28th - Monday

Nothing much happened all day. I chatted with some gunners who had come all the way from El Alemein, and a Welsh Guards sergeant told us (unofficially) that we were bound for Sicily.

June 29th - Tuesday

We were up at 5 o'clock and the whole assorted convoy moved off to SOUSSE where we went aboard LST 314, all vehicles reversing on with the four Ducks last. The theory is that IF the LST is damaged, and IF they are able to open the bow doors, and IF they can lower the ramp, the Ducks have a fair chance of taking to the water and making their escape. (Far too many 'ifs'). There are now 65 vehicles on our LST, 27 on the upper deck and 38 on the lower. We then join a convoy of seven other LSTs and, with an escorting destroyer, move off.

June 30ᵗʰ - Wednesday

On waking next morning there is no land in sight, but later on we moved back to the coast and moored off SFAX. I washed all my clothes but nothing else of interest happened all day.

July 1ˢᵗ - Thursday

In the early morning we went into harbour and moored alongside the quay. Again little happened for the rest of the day and in the evening we again moored outside the harbour. This strange 'to-ing and fro-ing' continued for several days.

July 4ᵗʰ - Sunday

Today was spent anchoring all the vehicles to the decks with chains and during the day 20 more LSTs arrive and we are all anchored out in the bay.

July 5ᵗʰ - Monday

Into harbour again and this time the rest of a gun crew came on board, also Jim. Again we move out and anchor in the bay. Another LST convoy arrives so that we now number about 60. The ship is now very full with men, vehicles and equipment. The heat is intense and this waiting is becoming very tedious for all concerned. A special anti-aircraft ship arrived equipped with two heavy guns, Oerlikons and multiple rocket-launchers.

July 6ᵗʰ - Tuesday

Today we take on board a team of Pioneers, who add picks, shovels and hammers to our tracking. Two of these hefty men are allocated to each Duck.

July 7ᵗʰ - Wednesday

In the early morning we move to a new position - the sea is choppy, and after boat drill, I write some letters.

July 8ᵗʰ - Thursday

The invasion of Sicily is now confirmed officially and at 4.30 p.m. the whole convoy sets off. We are one of 35 LSTs with 10 sub-chasers and several barrage balloons. I slept on deck.

July 9ᵗʰ - Friday

Next morning the sea is quite rough and I decide that I am not a good sailor! We are heading almost due east passing north of Malta, though we do not see it. In the evening I tried to get some sleep in the hold, but the noise of all the vehicles rocking in their chains was deafening, so I found an empty cabin and dozed off in a bunk.

SICILY

July 10ᵗʰ - Saturday

After a bad night I had no breakfast and repacked my kit. We seem to be in the middle of a huge armada of ships, but the only sign of any enemy hostility is a plume of black smoke on the horizon. The plan of campaign for the invasion of Sicily was as follows - The American 7ᵗʰ Army under General Patton was to land and capture the western part of the island, while the British 8ᵗʰ Army under General Montgomery would land and capture the eastern half. The enemy would then be pushed north and east until he was squeezed out of the island across the Straits of Messina. Here I should also quote an extract from Churchill's 'Second World War' Volume V, Page 26, concerning the invasion of Sicily.

> "For some time only the small ports of Syracuse, Augusta and Licata were likely to be available, and the armies would have to be supplied over the open beaches. This is successful largely because of the new amphibious load-carriers, the American D.U.K.W., and even more the Landing Ship Tank (L.S.T.) This type of vessel had first been conceived and developed in Britain in 1940. A new design based on British experience was therefore built in large numbers in the United States and first used in Sicily. It became the foundation of all our future amphibious operations and was often the limiting factor."

Facsimile of a map I carried all round Italy with me.

But back to the 10th. As we approached the island there seemed to be no signs of action (all the beaches had been cleared of the enemy some hours earlier by our initial assault troops), and when our LST was still some distance from the shore the bow doors were opened, the ramp lowered and the four Ducks took to the water. It was a bit choppy but quite navigable; however, two Ducks from another LST sank and their crews drowned together with a few Pioneers - the cause was unknown, but it was not from any enemy action. There were two possibilities, firstly the Ducks were overloaded, which is unlikely, or, secondly, a large drain plug in the bottom of the hull had been left out, allowing the water to pour in and the Duck would sink in a matter of seconds. This is the most likely explanation. Sadly we lost another Duck and driver the following day. We approached the beach at about 9 a.m. I forgot to mention that the whole assault operation was supported by the British Mediterranean Fleet, comprising six battleships, three aircraft carriers, nineteen cruisers and many destroyers and corvettes. Axis forces on the island were said to number eight Italian divisions and two German.

The beach was soft sand, but as our tyres had been deflated before leaving the LST, we had no problem. The beach was called Cap Passero on the extreme south/east tip of the island and we reported to the Beachmaster, a naval Petty Officer (all assault beaches are manned and controlled by the Royal Navy). Our tracking was quickly unloaded and we were directed to our parking area a short distance inland. At this point I quote from my diary -

"The country round this part is very barren and arid, being composed of very rocky soil and with no cultivation whatsoever, and criss-crossed with rock walls about two feet high."

We learnt that the initial landings had been made at 3 a.m. and by 6 o'clock all beaches were in Allied hands. Barrage balloons were flying, though there was no sign of enemy aircraft, but the constant drone overhead showed that the RAF was keeping a good watch and this continued throughout the day. Some areas of the beach were cordoned off with mine warnings. The rest of the day was spent ferrying stores from the RE dump to various beaches. We returned to our parking area about 9 that evening hoping for a good night's sleep; however a heavy air raid to the north-west meant that it was midnight before we could settle down. There was another short raid just before dawn.

EXCERPT FROM NEWS ITEM

When the Prime Minister last spoke of coming events, he referred to 'vast amphibious operations'. One of those operations was the invasion of Sicily and it was particularly apt that a major part in it should have been played by an amphibious weapon, the Allies' new DuKW lorries, whose secret had been well kept. These 3-ton 6-wheeled amphibians are being produced in large numbers for future operations. Equally at home on sea or land, their power unit is a lorry engine in every respect. Secret tests have been going on in America and Britain for some time, many RASC officers and men having been drafted without notice to undertake special training in the operation of the amphibians and when the invasion of Sicily was launched, the Ducks carried most of the munitions and supplies straight from the transport ships and landing craft to the fighting lines inland.

July 11ᵗʰ - Sunday

We were up about 7 and after breakfast it was my turn to take the first eight-hour shift. All yesterday we had been ferrying stores between dumps and the beaches, but today saw the first ferrying from ships. The procedure was as follows - myself and my two pioneers would report to the Beachmaster and he would direct us to a certain ship moored about half a mile offshore. At this point we would normally have two empty cargo nets in the hold. We would then 'drive' out to the vessel and manoeuvre alongside - if it was busy we might have to queue up with other Ducks to wait our turn. Once alongside, the pioneers would haul the two empty nets on to our rear deck and a derrick would lower a net full of supplies, ammo, petrol, rations, etc. into our hold and it would be guided to one end by the pioneers. They would then attach the empty nets to the derrick hook to be hoisted aboard. Then a second load would be lowered and guided into the other half of the hold. This was a full load and we would then head off for the beach. On shore the beach staff would see what we were carry-ing and direct us to the appropriate dump. On arrival the pioneers would unload the supplies by hand and we would then return to the beach with our empty nets and the whole process would be repeated until the end of our shift. We managed three loads that morning and then returned to the parking area about 2 p.m. and handed the Duck over to Jim and his two stalwarts. I was feeling a bit 'groggy' by now, but put it down to the after effects of the crossing. I lay down in some shade and felt too ill to move. About 6 I felt a bit better and managed to make my bed and, after eating a few biscuits and a cup of tea, I tried to get a few hours sleep; but an aerial battle developed overhead with spectacular anti-aircraft fire. At 9.30 p.m. when I was due to take over again, I was feeling much better and during the night we made five trips. The last one after the moon had set was tricky and several times I found myself trying to climb stone walls. A sharp air raid occurred about 5.30 a.m. (when I happened to be carrying a load of petrol), but the only casualty was a balloon that went up in flames over the beach. Any enemy plane is met with a hail of fire from both shore batteries and the naval ships that are patrolling offshore. Night bombers always drop flares before bombs, which light up the country for miles around, but these are very rare.

A Duck is loaded, whilst another (foreground) waits its turn
to draw alongside the ship.

'Monty' aboard one of our Ducks.

July 12ᵗʰ - Monday

Jim took over again about 7 a.m. and I am still feeling much better and even tried to eat a good breakfast from the cookhouse that is now in operation in one corner of our field. After a short rest I took over from Jim again about 2 p.m. - all the ships in the bay have now been unloaded, so we are now ferrying RE stores and equipment from one depot to another some miles to the north. We returned to our base at dusk, when air raids started all round us, but our beach escaped. As there is no more beach work at present, Jim stayed in camp that night.

July 13ᵗʰ - Tuesday

We were up at 8 o'clock this morning and found that during the night a large convoy of ships had arrived off our beach and Jim took the Duck and his team out to start unloading. By mid-morning I was feeling very ill again and this got worse as the day progressed. I lay down under a spare Duck and by afternoon was shivering yet pouring with sweat - this passed and during the evening I had a good meal, my first food all day, followed by a good night's sleep.

July 14ᵗʰ - Wednesday

I was up about 7 and after some breakfast took the Duck down to the beach on detail; but after two loads of petrol had to return to the park again as was feeling rotten. Jim took over and I again lay down under a Duck. By now I was feeling so ill that I packed my small kit and walked to the Field Dressing Station, where all I got was four pills to take before going to bed. I returned to camp and felt a bit better. I took the pills and bedded down; but the raids started again, so it was not a very good night.

July 15ᵗʰ - Thursday

Next morning I awoke and after a wash waited to see if the symptoms returned. At about 10 o'clock they started, so I again packed my small kit and personal belongings and was taken to a Field Hospital some miles to the north. After a short wait I went into a reception office and an officer asked me questions and took my temperature. It was 103.2 so he sent me to bed down in the general ward. This was a marquee with a large red cross. 'Beds' are stretchers laid on double tier wooden frames, about 40 in all.

I was given a pair of blue flannel pyjamas and climbed on to an upper tier. I was still feeling pretty rotten and glad to be able to relax, but during the night there was another raid.

July 16th - Friday

In the morning the old symptoms began again and an orderly told me it was malaria, but my temperature is now down to 101.6. I read a bit but dozed most of the day.

July 17th - Saturday

The same symptoms started again and during the morning we are told to get dressed as the Field Hospital is moving. After dressing I still feel ill, and after the usual delay we are all loaded into lorries and moved about 5 miles north to a place called Pachino. The hospital is now in a large building that used to be a Catholic school. After another wait about 20 of us are bedded down on stretchers laid out on the floor of a large hall. By teatime I felt a bit better and had a reasonable night's sleep.

July 18th - Sunday

After a bite of breakfast I had a good wash. I still felt a good deal better and there seems no recurrence of the high temperature. However I saw a medical officer who said he was sending me to the CCS (Casualty Clearing Station) at Syracuse for a blood test. I left in a lorry and arrived about teatime. This CCS is in a large block previously used as a mental home - there are small wards with six white metal beds in each, and a peep-hole in the door - very eerie. A very jovial RAMC Captain saw me soon after tea and gave me a thorough examination and asked me a lot of questions about my medical history. I was still feeling quite OK and after tea wrote some letters and bedded down. There was the usual raid during the night. I looked at my chart and it read - 'Malaria - query, Heat Stroke - query, Sandfly Fever - query' as apparently the symptoms are very similar for all, but my bet is malaria.

July 19th - Monday

I still feel OK, but have been put on 'fluids only' - so no breakfast, just some lime juice. I heard the news that a third of the island is now in the hands of the Allies. Later a major came round and when he asked me how I felt and I said, 'Fine,' he endorsed my chart 'feels fine - RTU' (Return to Unit). I spent the day wandering round and reading. I still felt OK, but a bit weak in the legs, probably due to five days inactivity. Later I saw the major again and persuaded him to put me on a normal diet. I had a good night's sleep.

July 20th - Tuesday

The MO says I can be RTU this afternoon. I packed my kit and left about 2.30. The officer at the gate had no idea where the 72nd was, but suggested I go to the Transit Camp 8 miles up the road. I hitch a lift in an ambulance, but the TC are no help either, but gave me two options - I could stay there indefinitely until I could be posted to a unit needing a spare RASC driver, or I could be given a 'Movement Order', authorising me to find my own way back to my unit. Of course in my mind there is no option, but as it is too late to make a start that day, I stayed in the Transit Camp for the night.

July 21st - Wednesday

I made an early start and after collecting my Movement Order, I decided to head south and try to reach Cape Passero in the hope that the Ducks might still be there, and I might meet up with one on the way. After several lifts I ended up at Pashino about midday. The Military Police thought the 72nd had moved out, but advised me to report to the Lighthouse Movement Control, who told me the Ducks were still operating. They gave me some biscuits and jam and I started walking south towards Cape Passero. On the way I met up with a Duck from another platoon who gave me a lift back to camp. Everyone seemed glad to see me again and, after I had reported back for duty, I had a meal, collected my back mail and relaxed. Jim arrived back from detail about 8 and greeted me in his usual quiet way. After swapping all our news, I volunteered to do the night shift and drove off about 2.30 a.m. The relief to be back in my old unit among my old buddies and driving my Duck again was immense after being adrift for almost a week.

July 22nd - Thursday

There is not much work now, so after two loads I returned to camp, and Jim took over about 6. Nearly all the ships have now gone and they expect the remaining ones will be emptied today. I had a good breakfast and repacked my kit. I took over from Jim about 1 p.m. and did three loads reporting back to camp about 8 o'clock. There is hardly any air activity now.

July 23rd - Friday

Our Duck is off duty today for painting and other maintenance. Later on we took it down to the sea to wash out the bilges and found the pumps not working, as usual. Back on site we heard the news that Palermo had fallen to the Americans. We bed down in the bivouac, which we can rig up in the hold of the Duck and I have my best night's sleep for ages.

July 24th - Saturday

We spent the morning continuing the painting of the hull and at noon Jim took her out on detail, returning at 8 p.m.

July 25th - Sunday

All beachwork has now finished and we are told that in the two weeks we have been here, 200 Ducks have ferried 19,000 tons of stores and supplies with only 28 working days lost through breakdown. Painting of the hull continued.

July 26th - Monday

Painting is continued, but during the morning I felt signs of the return of my fever, so lay down in the shade all morning. By afternoon I was perspiring freely, so bedded down in the Duck. I got up about 7 feeling a bit better.

July 27th - Tuesday

Once again I felt OK till mid-morning, but today the fever is not nearly so bad and I was able to take the Duck down to the sea to wash her.

July 28th - Wednesday

My symptoms seem to be fading, and I had an unexpected detail in the afternoon - Two LSTs have beached the other side of the bay and we are sent across to unload them.

July 29th - Thursday until August 11th - Wednesday

During this period our daily routine varies very little. After breakfast, maintenance on the Ducks continues in earnest, and of course during this time they are out of commission. We usually knock off about midday and after a meal we are free. We spend our time swimming, writing letters, reading and playing bridge. I have found three other bridge fanatics and we spend many pleasant hours in one Duck or another. There are very occasional air raids, but no one takes much notice of them. Apart from the intense heat, there are two other aspects of life that make it almost unbearable. First the flies -they swarm everywhere, and it is no exaggeration to say that, when eating, and lifting food on a spoon in the right hand, the left one must be used to wave over the food to prevent flies lighting on it before you can get it in your mouth. I have had a deep-seated dislike of flies ever since. The second was much more bearable - dust. I have already said that this part of the island has fine red sand and the Ducks raise this in clouds, so that one is always travelling in a cloud of pink dust and it gets onto everything and one ends up covered in a fine layer of the stuff. Of course swimming is a relief from both these scourges and we spend a lot of our time in the water. On the 11th we moved to a new location at NOTO, only about 20 miles north, and here the flies are not nearly so bad. We are parked in a field only a short distance from the town, so we are able to walk there, but it has little to offer, so we prefer to continue with our own amusements.

As everyone knows, the eternal stand-by of every soldier is the good old mug of tea and we always carried the wherewithal and 'brewed-up' whenever we had the opportunity. So it seemed only natural that we in 'A' platoon should choose the silhouette of a traditional teapot as the platoon's insignia, and it was painted in white on both sides of our Ducks underneath the serial number.

August 11th - Wednesday until August 25th - Wednesday

The above routine continued until the 25th when we moved on once again.

This time Jim and I are leading a convoy of 12 Ducks, each carrying a load of 160 4-gallon Jerricans of petrol. (When moving location, Ducks never travel empty.) We arrived at our night stop just south of Port Augusta, and watched a large convoy of LSTs travelling north along the coast. We slept on top of our load.

August 26th - Thursday

We continued north to CANTANIA. This had been the main Axis air base on the island from which raids on Allied shipping in the Med. had been launched. Jim and I are delayed by a puncture and while changing the wheel, we can see the many signs of the recent siege. The aerodrome is completely wrecked, either by shellfire or demolition, with not a building standing. We saw the wrecks of many German vehicles and minefields are clearly marked. Many planes are burnt out on the runways. When we caught up with our unit, they had already off-loaded their petrol at the local POL dump (Petrol, Oil, Lubricants), so we are told to retain ours to refuel our own Ducks. After a meal we went round each Duck filling them up, all this in the shadow of Mount Etna. We then continued about 8 miles further north to a village where 'Monty' had addressed troops that morning.

August 27th - Friday

After an early start (6.30 a.m.) we unloaded our empty cans and again moved north through a town called Mistabianca to our next stop. Here we are told that Jim and I with five other Ducks and their drivers and a corporal are to be attached to the Cameronians of the 5th Division. We also learn that, in the forthcoming invasion of Italy, we are to ferry the 6-pounder anti-tank guns immediately following the initial assault. The six of us move a few miles further north and meet up with our new companions, who will be our 'hosts' from now on. After a very good meal provided by the 'Laddies frae Scotland', we tidied up the Duck and bedded down.

August 28th - Saturday

After breakfast we give the Duck a final check and then stripped the rear deck of all fittings, spare wheel, spare petrol carrier, and anchor, in readiness for loading the gun.

August 29th - Sunday

Today we carried out our practice loading of the 6-pounder.

Noto - Sicily

Noto - Sicily

Our Duck was used as the experimental one, so it was watched by several of the Infantry Officers. Ramps were positioned behind the Duck leading up to the rear deck, then two short ones across the deck and lastly two more leading down into the hold. The winch cable was then passed forward through a pulley amidships and then back over the stern and attached to the front of the gun. As the winch was started the gun moved slowly forward onto the first pair of ramps, then up and onto and across the rear deck and then down into the hold. The first run was fine (apart from a ramp slipping onto my foot and a cable breaking!!!) - However we eventually had it loaded in the hold, but it was a tight squeeze - the hold was just wide enough to take the wheels, but the barrel of the gun projected forward over our shoulders and nearly reached the screen. However we had proved it could be done. This took all day and we finally bedded down in the Duck under the gun. There was an air raid on Port Augusta to the south during the night.

August 30ᵗʰ - Monday

The 5ᵗʰ Division comprises regiments from the Cameronians, the Wiltshires and the Inniskillens. Today we completed the loading of the Duck with ammo, water and rations and a light machine-gun, and prepared for our departure. The other three Ducks loaded their guns with little trouble, no doubt learning from our experience: the remaining two are being used as HQ vehicles carrying officers and HQ staff. We then leave for the Assembly Area a short distance away. In addition to Jim and myself, we now have the gun crew aboard, comprising two sergeants and four gunners, quite a load. The plan for the assault on the Italian mainland was as follows - the initial landings would be preceded by an intense artillery barrage across the Messina Straits, about 6 miles wide at this point. Once the beaches had been secured, the fleet of small surface craft would follow. The anti-tank guns of the infantry are usually towed by six-wheeled trucks called Portees carrying rations, ammo and water. These heavy vehicles could not be brought across the water till later, hence the Ducks.

August 31ˢᵗ - Tuesday

After a quick visit to the Duck workshops to cure a petrol feed problem, we trimmed the load, ammo, water, rations, etc. and left about midday. We took the coast road north but had to make many diversions owing to blown bridges. We could now see the coast of Italy quite clearly and our bombers were passing overhead all day going north. The final assembly area was a dried-up river bed (wadi) and there must have been well over 100 Ducks congregated there. We finally bedded down under the stern of the Duck this time, as by now, there was no room in the hold.

September 1ˢᵗ - Wednesday

Today we trimmed our camouflage net with strips of canvas; then Jim and I walked to the village, but there was nothing there, almost deserted, so we returned to our wadi and bedded down as before.

September 2ⁿᵈ - Thursday

Today I sent off my latest AML home and we left the wadi about 1 o'clock. Still travelling north to another wadi just south of Messina, arriving about 7 o'clock. Again all bridges had been blown, but we got an enthusiastic welcome from the local inhabitants. After a wash, shave and meal we are briefed by an RA officer about tomorrow's invasion. During the evening we watch as heavy guns move down to the beaches and we can see an intermittent glow from the mainland across the straits, probably enemy demolitions.

ITALY

September 3ʳᵈ - Friday

TODAY IS THE FOURTH ANNIVERSARY
OF THE OUTBREAK OF WORLD WAR II

and what a day it promises to be. We are shocked into wakefulness at 3.30 a.m. by the first guns and by 3.45 the barrage is in full swing. The noise is deafening, accompanied by the scream of shells and the sound of distant explosions across the water. The barrage stopped at 5.45 a.m. We had a good breakfast at 5 and moved off at 6. Our Duck, together with the other three 'gun' Ducks and two others, carrying the divisional platoon officers and HQ, go down to a small beach and into the water at 6.30. Our small convoy is in arrow formation - a naval motor launch guides us, followed by the two HQ Ducks, followed by the four gun-carrying Ducks - we are on the extreme right or south. The four Ducks carrying the guns must present a strange sight, sitting very low in the water, carrying a gun out of all proportion to their size - almost like miniature battleships. The crossing takes about an hour and a half and we pass many LSAs (Landing Ship Assault) returning after landing the infantry about three hours earlier. We are also passed by many LSTs carrying the reserve infantry brigade including Indian troops. The crossing is uneventful, apart from the odd shell passing overhead from our own artillery targeting some specific objective on the mainland. As we approach the coast we can see that the whole shoreline is shrouded in a thick pall of yellow brown fog, a mixture of smoke and dust raised by the earlier bombardment. This gives a most eerie atmosphere as we approach the beach. We land and drive up the beach at about 7.45, the first assault landing on the mainland of Europe after four years of war. An LCI (Landing Craft Infantry) is landing stretcher bearers, while a bulldozer is clearing a path through the trees to a lane beyond. We can hear mines being cleared as we drive our Ducks through the trees and along the lane for about half a mile, when the gun is quickly unloaded. We hitch it to our tow hook and then have some food. There is a brief visit from a few enemy fighters, but they get a very warm reception and soon clear off. At noon we are supposed to leave on a 'Mobile Patrol' but this is cancelled at the last moment - another brief visit from the Luftwaffe. At 3 p.m. we leave in convoy with the other Ducks plus the infantry carriers, mortars, Bren guns etc. We halt in a village just opposite the most northerly tip of Sicily - the gun is unhitched and trained up the road and our Duck is covered with its camouflage netting. At dusk a patrol that had gone on ahead returned - they had been in action against a German machine-gun post about a mile ahead. The gunners gave us a very good meal of bacon, fried potatoes, rice pudding, tea and biscuits. They also take over all guard duties, so we bed down in the Duck and have a good night's sleep.

September 4ᵗʰ - Saturday
Today we had a fairly easy time. We tidied up the Duck (yet again) - Spitfires are patrolling up and down the coast all day and we can hear explosions further up the coast, where the Germans

are carrying out more demolitions. The meals the gunners manage to produce are really excellent - don't know how they do it.

September 5ᵗʰ - Sunday

We are up at 6 and some time later a Bofors gun is mounted a few yards up the road. We all move off at noon in a sudden and unexpected rain shower. We park up for the night at Battalion HQ in a deserted village. During the night there was a violent and terrifying thunderstorm.

September 6ᵗʰ - Monday

We are up at 6 and dry out our blankets and erected the Duck's superstructure and repacked it, now under its tarpaulin. We move off again at about 2 p.m. in a very slow convoy - by 7 o'clock we have only covered about 4 miles. The convoy continued throughout the evening, passing through Seila and Palmi, a further distance of 25 miles. Driving conditions are horrific, sharp hairpin bends, no lights and over bridges only recently repaired by the RE. We park up for the night at about midnight at a place called Bagnara.

September 7ᵗʰ - Tuesday

We are up at 5.30 and after breakfast we are told that our gun is going forward to the front to hold a bridgehead over a river. At the last moment it is decided that Jeeps will tow the guns while we remain where we are. Don't know whether to be relieved or disappointed. They leave about 7.30 and we now come under fire from some German heavy 88 mm. Guns ('Whistling Willies') which causes an immediate response from a battery of our own 25-pounders mounted a short distance away. Soon after we move forward to a new area about 7 miles away, which we reach at about 9.30 p.m., where we park up for the night. We are told that our guns have been in action all day against a German machine-gun post, losing 5 carriers and 22 casualties. At 10.30 Jerry starts shelling the road a few hundred yards from us - one shell about every five minutes. Jim and I and Oswald, one of the gunners left behind, start digging a very good slit trench, fast - it is only shallow, but at least we can crouch in it below ground level. Of course just as we finish it, the order comes to move. We only move about a couple of miles, to another wood, possibly to escape the shelling. Here we find a slit trench already dug, so we bed down for the night beside it. We have no further disturbances during the night.

September 8th - Wednesday

Up at 7 and after a good breakfast, Oswald left us to rejoin his crew. We repacked the remaining rations and ammo in the Duck and moved off about 10. We passed through the village that had been taken the previous evening and the carriers that had been knocked out. Jim and I are now told that we are to take our Duck forward about a mile to a river which, with the bridge blown, is causing a bad hold-up of vehicles that cannot drive over the soft sand of the river bed. When we got there we found a few vehicles already stranded in the water, which was only about a couple of feet deep, with a long queue of assorted trucks, ambulances etc. lining up on the bank. They are the motorised transport of an infantry brigade consisting of 15 cwts, 3 tonners, portees, 6 pdr. guns. I was not too happy about our position, as we seemed to be in front of everything, right among the foot soldiers. We quickly deflated our tyres, drove into the water and began clearing the trucks that were stranded. With our special tyres and low gears the sandy bottom of the river presented no problem. We then parked on the far side of the river and, releasing our winch cable, Jim dragged it across and hitched it to the first truck, which was winched across until it could drive out. It was immediately very obvious that this method was going to take for ever, constantly winding and unwinding the winch cable, so we quickly abandoned it, and, letting out about 10 feet of the cable, locked the winch and, using it as a tow rope, began towing the vehicles across one by one. Jim would stand on the Duck or in the water doing the hitching and unhitching, while I did the driving. (Later we swapped over). This was much quicker and we made good progress. It must have been a strange sight, all these heavy, powerful vehicles queuing up helplessly immobile waiting to be towed across a small river with apparent ease by a strange monster called a Duck. At about 2 o'clock we were joined by two more Ducks and work proceeded much more quickly. Luckily we had no interruptions from Jerry and we learnt later that he had withdrawn earlier that morning. We towed the last truck across about dusk, when we stopped for some food and then drove back and joined up with the rest of our group. We felt we had done a good day's work, and the Ducks had really proved their worth. They had performed supremely well a task for which they were not primarily designed. On arriving back we heard that an independent brigade had been landed a few miles up the coast and are having a 'sticky' time. We also heard of the capitulation of Italy, and wonder what that will mean for us. After a meal we move to a new location about 5 miles away at a village called Mileto, where we spend the night. There was great rejoicing among the civilian population at the news of Italy's surrender.

September 9^{*th*} *- Thursday*

We are up at 6 and move up the road, where we park for a wash and breakfast. Shortly after one of our Ducks caught fire while it was being refuelled - fortunately it was not carrying any mortar bombs at the time, so we managed to control the blaze in the hold with extinguishers and soil - one lad was badly burned and had to be rushed to a Dressing Station. Unfortunately the bilges and engine were well alight, and when some small arms ammunition started to explode, we had to withdraw and watch it burn out. Poor old Geoff, the driver, had already sunk one Duck way back at Cap Passero. We moved on and joined up with HQ at a railway siding, where we picked up our gun and crew again. We also picked up a second crew - what a crowd. On again 20 miles to VIBO VALENTIA, where we have a great reception from the inhabitants. En route we pass some Seaforth Highlanders marching to the skirl of their pipes - stirring stuff. We finally parked up at some huge Italian barracks used by them as a store for ammunition. We then rewind our winch cable which had become tangled, had a meal and bed.

September 10^{*th*} *- Friday*

This is a quiet day - our advance units have failed to make contact with the Germans, who seem to be retreating fast. We spent the day exploring the barracks and sidings and picked up a big commercial fire extinguisher - with Geoff's blazing Duck still fresh in our minds, we thought it might come in useful, though we could not tell if it was still operative - we were later to find out. Our gun's portee arrived but there is no sign of us returning to our own unit yet.

September 11ᵗʰ - Saturday

The high spot of today is when 'Monty' addresses the troops in the barrack square, congratulating them on their success so far. This is followed in the evening by an ENSA concert with George Formby. Jim and I went into the town, but everywhere was shut, so we returned to camp and bedded down.

September 12ᵗʰ - Sunday

In the morning we transfer the gun and ammo etc. to the Portee - after the midday meal we say goodbye to our gunner hosts and travel south again, passing the shell of the burnt-out Duck on the way. We finally park up at a Stores Depot about 30 miles south of Vibo Valentia, where we take on a load of rations and spend the night.

September 13ᵗʰ - Monday

North again today to another dump near Vibo Valentia where we dropped our load and, after a meal, we pick up eight Italian officers and thirteen other ranks for transit to a POW camp at Reggio. It was a good run and we finally got rid of them and parked up for the night in the town square.

September 14ᵗʰ - Tuesday

We are up at 7 o'clock and are met by one of our own corporals on his bike, who leads us back to our own unit, after the two weeks detachment. They are also in Reggio (my diary records 'what a hole'). After our reunion we collect all our back mail and yet again tidy up the Duck and stow the tarpaulin. Later we picked up a load of our own troops and convey them to a wadi just north of the town. Later in the day I felt the old shivers coming on again and wondered if I was in for another bout of malaria. However the attack passed. Geoff, now Duck-less, is our permanent 'lodger'. Jim and I are on guard duty from midnight to 4 a.m.

September 15ᵗʰ - Wednesday

Four years ago today I joined up. Today we learnt that Monty requires a Duck for a couple of days for his own personal use. Jim and I very much hoped that we would be selected for this special detail, but, alas, this plum job went to another of the lads (see photo). After breakfast we are on detail at 'Howe Amber' beach carrying a load of Ordnance Stores to the Depot. Very smart Indian NCOs are in charge of Italian labour gangs, which they control with a 'rod of iron'. We carry a second load of MT stores and then a third of petrol. Our final load for the day is again RE stores and then back to the billet at 6.30 for a meal and an early night.

September 16th - Thursday

This was an easy day. Again we cleaned the 'Maid of Penzance', wrote up the diary and letters. I had my laundry done extremely well by a local resident. Platoon HQ arrives, at last, from Sicily.

September 17th Friday

I was up at 5 and at 5.30 was detailed (on my own) to collect 50 Italian POW from their barracks and take them to the BSD (Base Supply Depot) where they work as labourers. Back to camp for breakfast and a free morning, but at 1 p.m. I am again detailed to take a relief party of POWs to the BSD and return the original shift to their barracks. Back to BSD at 7 to repeat the lift.

September 18th - Saturday

Up at 7 and as there are no details, we take the Duck out to sea to give her a good wash down after the unsavoury loads of yesterday. Surprisingly we find the pumps are working. We return about teatime and the order to move comes at 5 p.m. We leave about 7 p.m. and pick up a load of ammo. (184 shells and charges for 25-pounders) We left about 11. This was a night drive, Jim driving while I dozed and slept.

September 19th - Sunday

We arrive about 10 miles north of Vibo Valentia about 7 next morning, but the ration truck is missing, so breakfast is delayed - it eventually turns up about 10. We leave again about 11 and on arrival at the dump, our ammo is unloaded by the Indian troops. Back to our location, where we bed down in the bivouac in the Duck, as this is supposed to be a bad malaria area.

September 20th - Monday

We move about 2 miles and park up in a small wood. We are free all morning, so write up the diary and more letters. Mid-afternoon we are on detail to unload a cargo of 'Compo' rations from a small schooner and move it to the DSD (Divisional Supply Depot). It is good to be on the water again after all the land carrying. I should explain here that 'Compo' rations are tinned and dried food packed in a stout carton, each containing enough food, etc. for one man for seven days, OR seven men for one day. They even include toilet paper, book of matches and a few cigarettes. All that is needed to provide hot meals is water and heat. This makes feeding troops on active service a matter of simple logistics. For example, 21 men are going out on detail for 10 days, i.e. 210 man/days - then they need to take 30 cases of Compo - easy. On this trip we see the remains of a crashed Spitfire.

September 21st - Tuesday

Another easy day - we go down to the sea and wash out the bilges and overhaul the bilge pump.

September 22nd - Wednesday

In the morning we unload a small Italian schooner containing supplies from Catania - back for a midday meal then to the ammo dump where we load up with 136 rounds of 3.7 Ack-Ack high explosive shells which are being ferried out to a Z boat off shore. When our turn comes it is too late to off-load, so we return and bed down on top of the shells. I am on guard with Jim from midnight till 2 and from 5 till 7.

September 23rd - Thursday

As the Z boat had now sailed our load is returned to the dump and again we take to the water to wash down and prepare for another painting.

September 24th - Friday

After breakfast we spent the entire day painting the hull - green decks, blue sides and green underneath, with black fittings - very smart. There is a rumour that we are moving to Taranto.

September 25th - Saturday

By midday we have finished painting and able to relax for the rest of the day.

September 26th Sunday

During the morning we help finish painting a neighbouring Duck and our move to Taranto is confirmed for the 29th. After dinner we load up with 184 rounds of 25-pounder shells - our watches are put back by one hour and it is now dark by 6.30.

September 27th - Monday

We spent the morning painting signs and talked for the rest of the day.

September 28th - Tuesday

We finished painting the signs and watch a violent thunderstorm out to sea. More bridge and chat - there was a sharp shower during the night.

September 29th - Wednesday

We are roused at 3 a.m., breakfast at 3.30 and moved off at 4.30. Our first destination is Crotone, but first we have to 'tow' another Duck from behind, as his brakes have failed. We rejoin the rest of the platoon at 10, when it stopped for a meal. Next we have a puncture and have to change a wheel - not too easy with a load of 3 tons to be jacked up. Spare wheels are now very scarce and we have to scrounge one from another platoon. We set off again and catch up with Mr. Joyce, one of our subalterns, and two broken down Ducks, one being towed by Wilf in A.22 (we are A.16). We take on the other, A.8., and after a tricky run, catch up with the rest of the platoon at Crotone. After a meal we bed down under our mosquito nets.

September 30th - Thursday

Up at 7 - we spend the morning mending the wheel. After lunch we report to some railway sidings for unloading - all the buildings are badly damaged - then back to base and after a short game of bridge, bed.

October 1ˢᵗ - Friday

We move off about 10, self driving and do about 80 miles north east towards Taranto. The only incident is when I misjudge a bend in the road and 'Maid of Penzance' ploughs through a stone wall, completely demolishing a large section of it. We get down to survey the damage, but all seems well and the hull intact; so, after moving several large boulders by hand, we are able to back off and continued our journey. We parked in a grove of trees for the night, but first we helped to jack up two Ducks and remove all twelve wheels, this being the only way we can obtain spares.

October 2ⁿᵈ - Saturday

We are up at 4.30 and leave at 6, Jim driving. We follow the coast road north-east towards Taranto and arrive at our location about 2.30 having done 90 miles without incident. The roads are really very bad, full of potholes and stones. After a meal we bed down for the night. There is a slight shower and some thunder during the night.

October 3ʳᵈ - Sunday

We are up at 6, but there is little doing. We play some bridge and then walk to the railway yards which seem to show little damage and trains are running quite frequently, (as they did all last night). After filling up at the PSP (Petrol Supply Point), we learn that Dennis, one of our bridge four, is leaving us. He is joining up with a special party of Motor Boat personnel. He is an awfully nice fellow and I shall be sorry to lose touch with him. We shall also miss his bridge prowess.

October 4ᵗʰ - Monday

We are up at 3 a.m. and leave at 5, self driving - we do 165 miles over very tortuous roads and tracks, amid beautiful scenery - there was one very bad diversion of about 5 miles where the rain had made the track very soft and it took us an hour to get through and even then we were one of the first out. We then did another 30 miles in the dark before arriving at out destination, SAPRI on the west coast about 9 p.m. There was no food, so Jim and I had to raid our own private supply of rations, which we kept hidden on the Duck.

We finally bedded down about 11.

October 5ᵗʰ - Tuesday

The morning is spent on maintenance and writing letters in the afternoon - as we are on guard duty tonight, we bed down at 7.

October 6ᵗʰ - Wednesday

I spent the morning tidying up my kit and playing cards in A.14 in the afternoon. We learn that we are now attached to 239 Company RASC, another Duck outfit, and all Ducks are now attached to the American 5ᵗʰ Army.

October 7ᵗʰ - Thursday

In the morning we cleaned out the filters and took A.16 down to the water to test the pumps. Cards again in the evening. There was a violent thunderstorm and rain during the night.

October 8ᵗʰ - Friday

We leave at 7 a.m., Jim driving, to go to a place called BELVE-DERE, 70 miles to the south on the coast, to collect petrol tins and drums - we arrive back about 6 o'clock, collecting a slow puncture on the way.

October 9ᵗʰ - Saturday

In the morning we changed our wheel - in the afternoon the rest of the platoon arrive, together with much back mail - the rest of the day is spent reading letters and bed at 10.

October 10ᵗʰ - Sunday until October 16ᵗʰ - Saturday

This week is spent on maintenance - we usually worked on the Duck till teatime and after our meal, settled down to bridge, reading and writing letters -there were several heavy storms during this period, but we are well protected in the Duck under the tarpaulin.

October 17ᵗʰ - Sunday

We are up at 6, and at 7 we go to the ammo dump to take on a load of 65 cases of 25-pounder shells and 32 cases of cartridges. We leave at 10.30. I rode Cpl. Wilkinson's bike into Sapri, where he took over and I joined Jim on A.16 and took over driving. We climbed to 2,800 feet in the first few miles and then took the inland road north for 90 miles. The country round here is much more cultivated and not so mountainous. Also the people seem

92

more civilised. At about 5 o'clock we were due to halt for the night - ours was the tenth Duck and at the top of a very steep incline the Ducks in front signalled that they were pulling off the road - I braked and the pedal went straight to the floorboards - complete brake failure - I instinctively hauled on the hand brake, but to no effect. On Ducks the handbrake is only a parking brake, the shoes only acting on the transmission shaft from gearbox to differential, so applying the handbrake was useless. Jim leaned across and kept his hand on the horn button to warn those in front that we were 'coming through' - we shot past with inches to spare amid much hand waving and shouting from the other drivers. By now we were doing about 40 m.p.h., and once we were clear of the others I could concentrate on how I was going to stop. I quickly realised that the only way was through the gears, but whether I could change down at the speed we were now doing was questionable, but there was no alternative; so with a silent prayer, I double declutched, screamed the engine and pulled on the gear lever. After a short grind it went home and our speed began to drop. I did the same through the other gears and, by the time I was in bottom, we were down to a crawl and I was able to bring A.16 to a halt on the grass verge. Both Jim and I heaved sighs of relief, but our troubles were not yet over. The handbrake had been hard on during our rapid descent and by now the linings had caught fire and were blazing away merrily underneath 3 tons plus of high explosive. Jim and I quickly removed the three floor gratings behind the driving cab and I grabbed the fire extinguisher we had nicked earlier and inverted it and with another silent prayer, banged the knob on the chassis. There was a hesitant hiss and suddenly a mass of white foam spurted from the nozzle which I directed on the flames and they were out in a matter of seconds. Then we really could relax and count our blessings. Another Duck had followed us down and parked behind us. After explaining what had happened, he hitched us up and towed us back up the hill to the parking area. All agreed that we had had a very narrow escape - to this day I don't know, if I hadn't managed to stop, whether Jim and I would have jumped clear and left poor old A.16 to its fate. After a meal Jim and I walked down the hill to see what lay ahead - it was horrifying. About a quarter of a mile beyond where we had stopped, the road took a very sharp turn to the left to avoid a sheer drop of about 100 feet - when we looked down we saw the base of this cliff was littered with the wreckage of trucks etc. that had not been as lucky as we had been. When we examined the Duck to see what had caused our problem it soon became apparent. The heavy rubber hose feeding brake fluid from the watertight hull to the rear of each wheel is held away from the tyres by a spring clip. We had omitted to attach one of these clips on one front wheel and as a result during the whole of our long journey north the edge of one tyre was rubbing against this hose, and when I braked hard at the top of the hill the extra pressure had caused the hose to burst with nearly fatal results. I don't usually say my prayers at bedtime, but tonight I made an exception.

October 18ᵗʰ - Monday

We were up at 6 - the rest of the convoy left at 7 and two fitters from workshops made a temporary repair to our brakes by isolating the axle with the burst hose until a new hose could be fitted. This left us with four-wheel brakes instead of the normal six, but quite adequate. We left about 10.30 and on good roads caught up with the convoy just outside Salerno. There is a terrible amount of damage all round, the result of the tragic landings a few weeks ago. We are now in the middle of the American forces, with troops and transport all around. We move on, Jim driving, and have our first view of Vesuvius, the Isle of Capri and the outskirts of NAPLES - we continue north to a place called NOLA, 10 miles north of the city, where we park up.

October 19ᵗʰ - Tuesday

We are up at 7 o'clock and go to an Ordnance Depot to get rid of our loads. Back to the parking area for our midday meal and at 2 o'clock we are detailed to take an advance party under Capt. Hitchin, with Sgt. Waite and thirteen men, into Naples to prepare our new accommodation, which is in an Italian barracks, a huge stone building in a very poor part of the city. It has no doors or windows, just wide openings in the end walls. We spend the rest of the day cleaning up and making the place habitable. We are to use six barrack rooms on the second floor, sleeping about a dozen men in each. There are a lot of planes about, all Allied and quite a few balloons. We bed down for the night in the Duck.

October 20th - Wednesday

We are up at 6 and I find a very good American flying jacket in a pile of salvage. We finish cleaning the rooms and the rest of the platoon arrives about 11 o'clock, and we set about settling ourselves into our new surroundings. I book my own and Jim's bed space in our dorm - the cookhouse and mess hall are on the ground floor at the back of the building. After our evening meal we listen to the radio and bed down in a building for the first time for many months. I think we all found the noise of a city very disturbing after the peace and serenity of our Ducks, usually parked miles from anywhere.

October 21st - Thursday

We are up at 7 and after breakfast we spend the morning taking down the Duck's superstructure and tarpaulin and generally preparing for another long spell of water-ferrying. I learn that I am to be sole driver of A.16 and Jim is in a pool of spare drivers. At present it is all night work and we will be working under the Yanks, unloading the Liberty cargo ships moored in the bay. These Liberty ships are pre-fabricated cargo ships of 10,000 tons and capable of 10 knots. They were built in large numbers all along the eastern seaboard of the United States. The various sections were fabricated in factories up and down the coast and then floated to assembly areas, where all the different sections were welded together, the engines installed and then fitted out. This unusual method of construction enabled them to be turned out very quickly and their numbers, carrying a vast amount of all types of war equipment, kept the Allied war machine in Europe fully supplied.

I helped Jim carry all his kit up to our new quarters and then got ready for my first night's detail in strange surroundings. After a meal I left about 7 with the other Ducks - on our way to the docks there is a sharp air raid - we stop and I get a scare when I see a cloud coming down the road towards us - GAS? - until I realise that it is a very effective smoke screen. The German planes drop flares and a few bombs, but none near us. The ack-ack is intense and we take cover under the stern of Geoff's Duck. We are stopped for a couple of hours and when the raid is over we move on down to the docks, which have been systematically demolished by the retreating Germans, before they were driven out

Naples panorama and Vesuvius.

Naples esplanade.

on October 1st. There is not a single berth where a ship could dock and consequently there is a fleet of cargo boats moored in the bay waiting to be unloaded. When we arrive at the docks they are brilliantly lit - the American policy is that night work continues under lights and these are only extinguished when an air raid warning is received. We arrive about 10 and just hang about for three hours, during which I find I have a puncture and have to change a wheel. We are finally dismissed about 1 o'clock, having done no work at all and return to our barracks at about 2 a.m.

October 22nd - Friday

We are up about 7 and I spend the morning rewinding the winch cable and we move all the Ducks to a new parking area. I rest during the afternoon, as am on detail again at 7 o'clock. This time when we leave the barracks, we do not go to the docks, but are parked in a lane leading down to the Duck beach, or 'hard', as the Americans call it. We are in a long line of Ducks, mostly American, distinguished by the large white star stencilled on both sides. We crawl forward slowly and just before midnight I reach the 'hard', controlled by Yanks and am directed to a ship some half mile off shore. I enter the water and head for my target - Naples Bay is vast and there are about 50 ships at anchor. As no air raid warning has been received, the docks about half a mile away to my right are brilliantly lit, but this only serves to contrast the blackness of the water and the outlines of the ships, with the silhouette of Vesuvius with its glowing crater outlined against the night sky. I reach my ship and take on board two net loads of ammunition - but now I have no idea where the Duck 'hard' is - unlike the docks, it shows no lights and I get hopelessly lost. At one scary point I find myself driving among the masts and superstructure of a sunken ship, and have another fright when I notice a red glow between the cracks in the floorboards of the cab - is she on fire, again? - On investigation I find it is only the exhaust manifold which is glowing red hot - apparently this is quite normal when the engine has been running at full throttle for a long period. After much hunting I eventually find the 'hard' and am told to take my load to a railway siding, where it is off-loaded on to a train. I return to the 'hard' - this time I am sent by road to the docks to transfer a load of mixed stores from a quay to a Class

I dump - back to the docks about 6 and I see them in daylight for the first time. The damage is truly complete and extensive. I return to the barracks about 7.

October 23rd - Saturday

I work on the Duck during the morning and in the afternoon Jim and I walk into Naples - my diary reads - "I am not at all impressed with this city and it looks very like all the other Mediterranean towns we have seen, except that there is a better class of goods in the shops than we have seen so far." I bought an electric torch in a shop and Jim bought a second-hand watch from an Italian. We get back about 5 and have our meal. There is a short air raid and we bed down about 8 o'clock, as my night details have now been switched to days.

October 24th - Sunday

Up at 6 and on detail at 7 - it is a good day's work - one load of Engineering stores to Yale dump, another of ammo to Kelly, another of stores and then one of petrol (during which I hit a submerged wreck, fortunately with no damage) another of ammo, and finally a load of gas stores - I refuel and return to barracks about 6 and so to bed.

October 25th - Monday

There is a parade on the roof of our barracks at 8.30 and then we were free for the rest of the morning. On returning to our Ducks after lunch we find they have been systematically looted - all our personal possessions have gone, my glasses, sun glasses, torch, watches, tins of fruits, jack knife, a can of gas - we are all furious and our opinion of Italians, never very high, hits rock bottom, but there seems little we can do. I have a haircut and shampoo and then rigged an extension to the gear level of A.16 - serves no useful purpose really, just a gimmick. I also buy myself a yachting cap a la Churchill, which I now sport whenever I am on detail. I am on guard with 'Loftie' from 10 - 12 and 4 - 6. There is an alert during the night with flares and explosions from the docks - we find out later that it was an E-boat attack.

October 26th - Tuesday

Today we caught two of the young Italians who robbed our

Naples

Ducks yesterday and 'persuaded' them to take us to their 'dwell-ings', two filthy rooms which we search at revolver point assisted by the Italian police, but found nothing. So we returned to the Ducks. Jim is called out on detail on A.21 and I helped clean our billets. I am called out with six others at 11 a.m. and we carry two loads of petrol and one of ammo - back at 6.30 and bed at 7.

October 27th - Wednesday

We spent the morning on maintenance and in the afternoon walked into Naples and did some shopping to replace some of the stolen articles. There is some ack-ack fire and I am back at the billet at 4 and on detail again at 7. Three of us stayed together, Harry Cook on A.14, Vic Caves on A.15 and self on A.16. We carried two loads of petrol from 'Gillian' and one of K rations (American equivalent of our Compo) from 'Brackstone', Peter Gorman on A.18 broke down and I had to tow him to the petrol dump. Harry Milton on A.12 lost a wheel in the water - back to billet at 6 a.m.

October 28th - Thursday

Spent the morning on maintenance and after lunch did some laundry and had a shave at a barber's. There was a severe electric storm at teatime. Back to the 'hard' on detail at 7.30, still raining, picked up a load of 8-inch shells from 'Bartlett' after a long wait with Peter Gorman on A.18 (now repaired). We see the wreck of a Yankee Duck on a salvage barge. Our shells are unloaded at a railhead and after further delay we are sent out to collect some personnel from 'Astra', but found they had already been collected. Back to the billet at 6 and after a meal bedded down.

We soon found that a horizontal length of the exhaust pipe in the engine compartment was ideal for heating tinned food. One day, anticipating our lunch break, we put a tin of Machonochie (meat and veg. Stew) in the usual place to heat up. During the morning's work there was a loud explosion from the engine com-partment and I immediately realised what had happened - we had forgotten to pierce the tin before putting it on to heat - sure enough, on opening the engine hatch there was no sign of the tin - it had exploded, covering the engine and surroundings with a rich layer of meat, vegetables and gravy - I don't think we ever got rid of the subsequent smell.

As this day-to-day-diary is becoming very repetitious, I will revert to narrative.

We spent the next two months up to Christmas in Naples and in the same barracks, doing the same day or night, ferrying all types of stores and supplies from ships to depots with occasional guard duties. During this period we fed like lords - if our cook wanted anything extra he tipped us the wink and one of us carrying rations would make a diversion to our cookhouse - at one point he had two three-tonners filled with American rations. I also had a case of tinned fruit hidden in the bilges of A.16 in case I felt thirsty. During this time, I had two unusual loads - two portable generators and twelve 500 lb. aerial bombs. There were still occasional air raids on the docks, but repairs to the berths went ahead rapidly. Unloading ships by Ducks was essential and could not be disrupted, but was very slow and it was imperative to be able to berth ships in the docks as quickly as possible.

On November 21st, I and a few others attended a symphony concert at the famous San Carlo Opera House, a magnificent building and the concert was equally impressive. On December 15th the hospital ship *Dorsetshire* anchored in the bay. I last saw her moored on the river Dart in Devon in the summer of 1939 while I was on holiday in Dartmouth.

On December 23rd work for our platoon ended, and the Ducks returned to Nola for the usual spell of intensive maintenance. On Christmas Day I was not feeling too well, but managed to do justice to the magnificent dinner our cooks had produced (thanks to our American friends). It was traditional turkey with all the trimmings, followed by plum pudding. But I was very sick later that night. On Boxing Day I still felt pretty rotten, so stayed in bed all day. Bert Addison, the Q clerk from another platoon, came to see me and said he had suspected jaundice, so it looks as if I may have it too. We decided to report sick the next day. However the MO sent us back to barracks and we are to report again in two days' time. When we got back to our billet we found all the others had moved out to Nola and it was nice and peaceful after the very rowdy Christmas celebrations. Bert moved his bed next to mine and from now on he is my new 'buddie' - he is a nice chap from Bristol and was in charge of our petrol pumps in Westerham. Although I could not know it at the time, I was destined never to see Jim or the Ducks again.

Modern post-war Ducks in training.

On the appointed day Bert and I reported to the MO again. He confirmed that we both had jaundice and wrote a note to the CRS (Casualty Receiving Station). We return to the barracks and pack all out kit and are taken to the CRS at about 2 o'clock. It is a requisitioned civilian nursing home, still run by Italian staff and is very comfortable. We are received by an orderly and shown into a bedroom with five beds, but no other patients - we choose two beds and settle ourselves in. It is all very professional and spotless. We read and talk for the rest of the day, and are brought boiled eggs for tea at 8 p.m. The sister, a charming lady who speaks excellent English, arrives and is most apologetic, as no one had told her of our arrival. We settle down to sleep about 9.30.

Next day all our meals are fish, but very nicely served - in the afternoon we have a visit by the ADMS (Assistant Director of Medical Services), a genial old colonel, who asked us a lot of questions - another patient from REME (Royal Electrical and Mechanical Engineers) arrives, also with jaundice, or, to give it its proper name, Infective Hepatitis. Next day two more patients arrive and a lad from our unit visits us and brings us some mail. It is all very pleasant and relaxing but I would much prefer to be back with the lads and the Ducks. I teach Bert Bezique and he tries to teach me the rudiments of chess.

Bert Addison.

1944

The New Year arrives and this respite from the war continues until my 28th birthday on January 10th. On the 12th Bert is discharged to a Convalescent Depot and a Canadian takes his place. During the whole of this time all my waking thoughts are centred on how to get back to my mates and the Ducks once I am released. I realise that at present things are out of my control, so all I can do is await developments. On the 13th I hear that my unit had moved to Salerno - I receive some more mail, also the rest of my kit, including my Lilo, my most precious possession. On the 14th we are all moved to a 10-bed ward, not so comfortable or luxurious but not too bad. On the 16th I am up and about and am told that I go to the Convalescent Depot tomorrow. I have a visit from Les Wilson, who is the MT clerk from another platoon. He tells me that our two Duck platoons are being amalgamated and are to become part of 239 Company, another Duck unit - the surplus men are returning to the old 72 Company. My secret plan therefore is that when I am finally discharged from the Con. Depot I try to report to 239 Coy. and hopefully join up with the old crowd again. Next day I pack all my kit and, with two other lads, am taken to No. 7 Convalescent Depot at Sorrento, which we reach at 1 o'clock. Then follow all the formalities of checking in, pay checks, documentation etc. etc. It is a vast place, catering for several thousand troops from every kind of regiment. The jaundice epidemic that hit the Middle East Forces at this time was widespread and must have caused huge problems for those in command. I am in No. 2 division, Z Company, No. 874. We then go to Z Coy. office, where we are again booked in and then taken to our billet, a ground floor room in an empty hotel overlooking the Bay of Naples with Vesuvius still smoking in the background - our room has a terrace with a sheer drop to the water, a truly magnificent vista. We go to a large communal dining room and learn our new routine, which is very relaxed, no guard duties and only very light fatigues. I repack my kit, putting all my most treasured possessions, (including Lilo) in my kit bag, which I can lock. Then three of us go for a walk in the town, much the same as any other Italian holiday resort, except that the trams are running. The goods in the shops are very shoddy. The daily routine is easy,

No.7 Convalescent Depot, Sorrento - view from our bedroom.

short route march, medical grading, lectures on VD (!), light fatigues. (I find myself raking the flower beds in the public square in the centre of the town - thank God for a sense of humour!) I have tried to find Bert with no success so far. Capt. Hitchin, one of our officers is also a patient here (it seems that disease is no respecter of rank).

On January 18th, after breakfast and roll call, there is a dental and medical check and I am graded II with light duties. I see Capt. Hitchin and he tells me that the Ducks have left Naples and are at Salerno already loaded up for an imminent operation, so it seems that my chances of joining up with them again are vanishing swiftly. Capt. Hitchin says he hopes to be discharged on Friday, two days away and will take me back with him to the old 72nd Coy. if I am pronounced fit to go. On Friday, the 21st, I meet up with Bert again and we swap all our news. A huge flight of Flying Fortresses passes overhead flying north and a large convoy of assault craft and LSTs leave Naples - we later learn that this is the commencement of the Anzio landings further up the coast behind the German lines and just south of Rome, in which the Ducks are heavily engaged. And with that convoy goes my last hope of meeting up with my beloved Ducks again. On the 23rd Capt. Hitchin saw the MO and arranged for me to be graded 'I - fit for discharge'. He is taking Bert and myself with him by car tomorrow to rejoin the old 72nd Coy. now stationed in the southern part of Italy.

Although I took no part and knew nothing about it at the time, perhaps a few words about the abortive assault at Anzio might be of interest. The German Gustav line stretching right across Italy with Monte Cassino at its centre, was proving to be a tough nut for the Allies to crack. So General Alexander planned a secondary amphibious attack at the rear. The place chosen was the small port of Anzio, about thirty-five miles south of Rome on the west coast of Italy. The object of the assault was twofold: firstly it would cause a diversion for the German forces and cause them to divert men and armour from the main front, and secondly, as soon as a sufficient force had secured a bridgehead it was intended that it should strike out to the east to cut the enemy supply and communication lines and hopefully take the Germans by surprise. Unfortunately it did not turn out that way. The American general in command of the bridgehead spent too long 'digging in' and building up his forces - this took two days and this was all the time the Germans needed; so when eventually the breakout was launched it was met with fierce resistance from reserve German divisions rushed in to contain the bridgehead - and thus the opportunity was lost and the Gustav line was not finally broken until May.

Southern Italy

On Monday, January 24th at the Convalescent Depot Bert and I are up early, as we are due to meet Capt. Hitchin at 9.30. We pack all our kit and hand in our blankets (I manage to keep a very good American one). We meet as arranged and find there is a third passenger, a Sister from the QAIMNS (Queen Alexandra's Imperial Military Nursing Service), also moving south to her hospital in Bari. We leave about 10 in a staff car that Capt. Hitchin has organised from a pool. I drive and he sits beside me as navigator, with Bert and the Sister in the back. We head south, and so it is goodbye to Naples and the Ducks, and a new phase in my army life is about to begin.

We pass through Salerno, but there is no sign of 239 Company or the Ducks. We have a good run and arrive at Potenza about midway between the two coasts of Italy, at 5.30. We drop Capt. Hitchin and the Sister at the Officers' Hotel and then take the car to some RE barracks, where they give us a meal and we have a good night's sleep. Next morning we are up early and, after filling up with petrol and oil, we meet Capt. Hitchin and the Sister at their hotel. We have another good run south to the Adriatic coast, which we follow down to Bari, arriving about 1 o'clock, We drop the officers at their club and then Bert and I go and have a meal at an Italian Restaurant. After lunch we collected them again and dropped the Sister off at her hospital, then carried on south to San Vito, about 10 miles outside Brindisi, arriving about 5 o'clock. This is where the rest of 72 Company is now based. We dropped Capt. Hitchin at the Officer' Mess and then report to 'C' platoon billet where we are sleeping. Here we meet up with many old friends whom we have not seen since landing in N. Africa, which seems like light years ago. There is much news to exchange. Bert and I report to the CSM next morning -

we are posted to 'B' platoon and on arrival at their billet we report to 2/Lieut. Gale, and I find myself once again the 'Q' clerk for his platoon. We are billeted in what is a private bird sanctuary - there are many exotic birds in cages with several peacocks strutting around quite freely, including a pure white one.

The main stores are in a marquee, but I have my stores-cum-bedroom in the basement of one of the buildings. The next week is spent getting my office and stores organised to my liking and settling down to a routine that is all too familiar. For relaxation we can go into Brindisi, where there is a good NAAFI and a cinema showing English films, unusual for these parts; we have had some snow, also unusual, and the weather is very cold. Lighting is a bit of a problem, especially in my dark basement, as the civilian mains supply is very erratic, but we improvise by running a dynamo off the rear wheel of one of the Bedford trucks.

On February 10th I received a message that I am to be transferred to Workshops to train as a TMT clerk - this is similar work, but deals only with transport spares and equipment. So next day, yet again I pack my kit and hand the stores over to Bert and am taken to the Workshop billet, where I meet my new mates, though of course I have known most of them for a long time. Next day the MSM (Mechanist Sergeant Major) tells me to work with Bob Scott - I was not at all happy about this transfer, and it only took a few hours for me to realise that the new work is tedious in the extreme and will bore me stiff, so I set the wheels in motion.

First I speak to a senior corporal 'Waf' Turner, whom I know well and ask him to speak to Capt. Parker, the Workshop officer, about my possible return to 'B' platoon. I also see Lieut. Gale and it seems that no one was consulted about my move. A few days later I put in an official application for transfer back to 'B' platoon - Capt. Parker saw me and said he had agreed to my application and in return I agreed to stay on until a new workshop stores section was established. This took a week and then Capt. Parker told me that I am returning to 'B' platoon tomorrow. I returned in triumph the next day and Bert handed the stores back into my care again, and we all settled back into our usual routine. As long as I do the job efficiently no one bothers me and I am my own master, which was certainly not the case in Workshops.

Brindisi submarine base.

Brindisi maritime war memorial.

Early in March I had to report to the MO with a badly ulcerated throat, but a few sulphanilamide tablets soon cleared it up. There was one momentous event - I am promoted to Local/Acting/Unpaid Lance-Corporal yet again, for the third time!!!

During this very uneventful period I manage to do quite a bit of driving, usually in the 15 cwt. or Chevrolet truck on official (or unofficial) work connected with the stores. Once I had to take one of our chaps to a CMP (Corps of Military Police) Depot to serve 14 days Field Punishment for some misdemeanour. We have a lot of free time and it is spent writing letters, playing board games and almost daily visits to the Brindisi cinema, but the films on offer are pretty second-rate as a rule. Of course I am still exempt from all guards and fatigues, but I do miss all the activity and excitement of the Ducks - I have had no word of them since we left Naples. The weather is cold and wet, not a bit what one would expect from a Mediterranean climate. At the beginning of April the weather improved and we organised some cricket matches amongst ourselves. I took a truck to the local RE dump to try to scrounge some matting for our pitch, and we cut down three trees that were obstructing the outfield.

In the middle of April we move to a new location, where my stores is a room in a wooden building, where I also sleep and is much more comfortable than my dingy basement. The drivers bed down in their bivouacs. The old routine continues. I am able to borrow one of the corporal's bikes and so get out quite a lot. I make several trips to a local bomber base, hoping to cadge a flight - I have never yet been up in a plane - but so far without any success. My duties are still domestic, issuing the free cigarettes and green envelopes, making out pay acquittance rolls and supervising pay parades, exchanging clothing etc. I also get in a small stock of NAAFI goods, chocolate, writing paper, pens, etc., which I sell to the lads (at a small profit to myself, of course).

On April 29th my perseverance is rewarded and I manage to get a flight. I was touring round the base on Cpl. Knibb's (Nibbie) bike and saw the crew of a Halifax bomber preparing to take off. It turned out they were Polish and none spoke any English - however, I managed to make them understand that I would like to go up with them, to which they readily agreed. (I assumed that they were going to return to the same base). It seems they were going

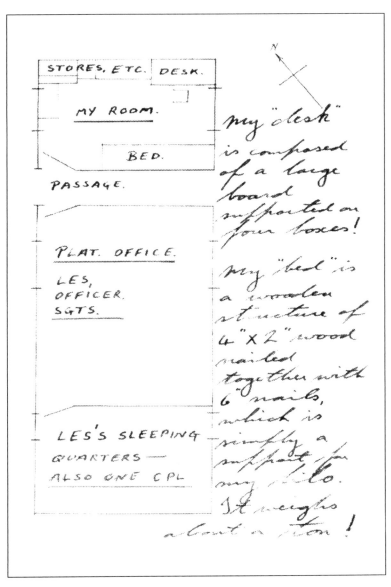

Plan of offices - April 1944 - sent home in a letter.

on a short test flight after some servicing - it was a great thrill - we flew out over the Adriatic and saw the coast of Albania, then south over Taranto and back to base.

During this time the unit is moving cargo from the docks at Brindisi to the dumps and about this time our old Bedford lorries are exchanged for American Dodges. I manage to get out driving on detail as Les Wilson, my opposite number in charge of transport, will put me out whenever I ask. On one of my visits to the air base a Liberator bomber had crashed on landing and burst into flames - I took the bike and went to have a look - fortunately all the crew had managed to escape. Apparently it was taking supplies to the Yugoslav partisans and developed engine trouble and had to turn back. It crashed on landing - the crew managed to get out and water tankers arrived to try to quell the flames, but the plane was also carrying mortar bombs and when they started to explode everyone had to retire.

In mid-May a stray puppy 'adopted' me and took up residence in my hut. I made it a bed, but it was not happy, so it ended up in bed with me.

In mid-May we had another move, this time to a place called 'Paradise Camp', but still in the same area. Again my store is in a comfortable hut and puppy and I soon settled in. This is a somewhat hush-hush place - we are attached to an RASC unit called ME 54, which simply stands for Military Establishment. It is a large depot which packs the parachute containers with food, arms first aid, etc. to be dropped by parachute to the Partisans in Yugoslavia. Our job is ferrying all these stores from the various dumps to the depot for packing and then taking the packed containers to the planes on the nearby base. I learn that they are looking for volunteers to fly in the planes (DC 47s, Liberators and Halifaxes) as despatchers and help unload the containers from open hatches over the target. I was also told the work can be hazardous. I briefly (very) think about having a go, but the thought of Sheila and Michael waiting for me back home soon puts me off the idea. So far this month, we are told, 1000 tons of supplies have been dropped, thus keeping 22 Germans divisions engaged in the Balkans. I later heard that during one 'drop' (obviously always at night) three DC 47s had collided - two broke up and the third fell in pieces - it seems my decision was right after all.

Les Wilson has moved into the hut with me - he is now dealing solely with MT details, so much of his previous work now falls to me. Sadly my puppy has disappeared. At this time I make myself a new bed with a stout wooden frame and canvas base and found it more comfortable than my trusty Lilo, though it weighs a ton. Transporting it is no problem - it simply goes in with the stores.

On May 27th, a group of us go to see 'Madame Butterfly' at the local opera house - a very good production though in Italian. The next day HQ, Workshops and 'D' platoon move out to a new location near Bari, some miles to the north, but whether we are to follow is not yet known. On June 1st we do move out to join the others. We pass through Bari, a big bustling city and on to San Spirito, a small seaside holiday resort about 10 miles north of Bari. The city has many fine buildings and both Britain and America have many headquarters there. It has a very strong anti-aircraft defence. In San Spirito my office/cum/store/cum/bedroom is the ground floor of a small whitewashed villa on the seafront. Les has his office in a similar one a few doors away. On June 6th we hear on the radio of the long-awaited D day landings in Normandy, also the capture of Rome. Following our latest move the unit is now clearing stores etc. from the Bari docks, which are much more extensive than those at Brindisi, to the dumps. In order to increase the load-carrying capabilities the unit is issued with Hobbs trailers to tow behind the Dodges.

June 7th is another 'black' day in the army career of L/Cpl. Bennion. I took (quite legitimately) a covered 3-ton truck into Bari to collect the free issue cigarettes and some NAAFI supplies for the unit. One arriving back I found that 54 tins of cigarettes and 59 bars of chocolate had been stolen from the back of the truck. It must have happened while I was stopped in heavy traffic coming out of Bari. One 'Eyetye' must have climbed over the tailgate, through the tarpaulin flaps and passed the loot to his mate waiting in the road below. I reported the theft as soon as I got back, but two days later the blow fell - 'L/Cpl. Bennion charged with losing by neglect a quantity of cigarettes and chocolate' - Verdict - Guilty - Sentence - 'Reduced to the ranks and 21 days Field Punishment' - I was absolutely shattered at this latest twist of fate. However, the CO called me into his office afterwards and said that he was sorry to have had to give me such a severe

San Spirito.

sentence, but he had no alternative. He added that he knew I was doing a good job in the platoon and that, as far as the 21 days F.P. was concerned, he felt my duties would keep me pretty well occupied, so I would serve my sentence doing my usual duties. Naturally I felt very bitter at being punished so severely for something I felt I had no control over and vowed that, as soon as my sentence was over, I would put in for a transfer. There was an interesting aftermath to all this. On the evening after my 'trial' I was summoned to appear before a Court of Enquiry to be chaired by Capt. Edwards to find out how a quantity of cigarettes and chocolate came to be missing in transit. When I told the Captain that I had already been charged, convicted and sentenced for the affair, he was astounded and said that it put him in the difficult position of being able to over-rule the CO's verdict. Of course he didn't, but it was a classic case of an army 'cock-up' - the Court of Enquiry should have been held first, and any further action based on its findings. In all this I consider I was the innocent victim.

A few days later, while still serving my 21 days, I asked Les to put me out on night detail - but cruel fate had not quite finished with me yet. On returning empty (no trailer) to the Report Centre at the docks, I was coasting slowly up behind the Dodge parked in front, and, for some unknown reason, in a fit of mental aberration, I switched off the engine before I stopped. I forgot that this also switched off the power brakes, so when I went to stop, I didn't, and slid gently into the rear of the other truck. The damage to Vic's truck was minor, only a bit of splintered woodwork, but my radiator was pushed back onto the fan. I got towed back to Workshops and Les got me a replacement and I completed the detail. When I put in the accident report I just said 'partial brake failure' - and naturally didn't mention switching off the engine. However when he saw the report Capt. Parker said 'he did not accept my statement', which was fair enough. And so, two days later I am up before the CO yet again, this time charged with 'damage to WD vehicle by careless driving'. By this time I had had enough, so decided to be awkward and asked to be tried by Court Martial. I think the CO must have taken pity on me, because he said that, if I agreed to let him try my case, he would be lenient - I was very tempted to ask him 'How lenient?' but decided that discretion was the better part of valour, so agreed and was 'Admonished' - which, again, was fair enough. Though I did wonder afterwards if the thought of all the paperwork and hassle of a Court Martial might have influenced his decision.

As these times are so uneventful (apart from the above), I might write a word or two (or three) about money. With the capitulation of Italy, control of all aspects of Government was taken over by AMGOT (Allied Military Government of Occupied Territory) and one of the first things done was the issue of military currency in the form of special notes printed in the currency of the country, Lira. These quickly became the main currency for all transactions and were accepted everywhere - but only within the boundaries of Italy - outside, this currency was worthless. This posed a problem for anyone who had amassed a fortune, large or small, by fair means or foul - how to transfer it to the UK. There was one small legal loophole which was exploited to the full. Army Post Offices in all big cities had stocks of the good old English Postal Order in one denomination only, £1, and these could be bought over the counter for the military lira in the normal way, at the fixed exchange rate of 400 lira to the £1. This loophole was controlled by restricting the sale to two postal orders per man per day, and of course these could then be posted home in the ordinary way quite legitimately. The result was that from the time the APO opened its doors first thing in the morning till closing time, there was a long line of servicemen queuing up to buy their ration of Postal Orders. Of course I was one of the queue many times and sent my POs back to my bank in England in batches of twenty regularly. One amusing outcome - when I eventually got home and looked at my bank statement, I was amused to see many debit entries marked 'poundage on out of date postal orders' - I wonder what the manager made of it.

My usual routine of store duties interspersed with night details on the docks continued throughout July. (I ended my 21 days F.P. on June 30th.) On July 16th another incident occurred which is worth recalling, and which might have had serious consequences for me. The labour on the docks was all Italian and one night when I was on detail, one of them intimated that he would like to buy my boots. Of course I needed them myself, but I made him understand that if he met me tomorrow night I might be prepared to do a deal. So next night I 'borrowed' a pair of new boots from my stores and took them with me to the docks. I met my 'friend' and showed him the boots and he was delighted, but explained that he did not have the money on him, but if I took him home he could get it. It sounded a bit fishy to me, but, thinking his home was just round the corner, I agreed and he climbed in beside me. He guided me for what seemed an age, right out of Bari and I was beginning to get worried on two counts - firstly I could be being led into a trap, have all my belongings stolen and my throat cut - and secondly, and even worse, I could run into a Military Police Patrol and even my fertile imagination would not be able to explain how I came to be so far off my authorised route and carrying an illegal civilian. However, neither of these things happened; so, after 30 miles (!) of driving down dark lanes, we came to his village and I was at once surrounded by a sea of smiling faces. Money was produced and the deal completed (I got 800 lira for the boots), and I was pestered to fetch some more. At the time I was carrying a load of dunnage, worthless scrap timber used in cargo holds as packing round shells etc. - they even wanted to buy that, offering me 10,000 lira for it. But by now I was getting cold feet - I still had to get back to the docks without being picked up; so I explained by gesture that perhaps next time, and they seemed happy. My 'customer' then guided me back to the safety of the docks without incident and we parted good friends. But I shudder to think what might have happened and vowed to be much more careful in the future. (note - the books were easily 'cooked' to account for the missing boots.)

On July 21st the CQMS asks me if I would like to return to HQ platoon as his clerk, but I feel I am quite happy as I am, so say sorry, but no.

August passes and September 3rd marks the fifth anniversary of the outbreak of war and on the 15th the completion of my five years in the Services.

And so September and October pass in much the same way with little of interest to report. An Italian cadre is added to the platoon and I had the job of enrolling them and keeping their records. I had a very good Italian 'odd job' man who spoke quite good English and he acted as my interpreter - I had to make out their muster rolls for the weekly pay day, and if one or two fictitious names appeared, who was to know!

I was out on detail most nights and on my stores duties during the day - I found I could manage with very little sleep, and enjoyed the variety and independence my duties allowed.

One unusual three-day detail I went on was transporting the Royal Armoured Corps Band, and all their instruments - from Bari, where they had been giving a concert, to Taranto. It took three 3-tonners to carry all the men and their equipment.

In October we all changed from summer khaki drill to the regulation battle-dress - more work for the 'Q' clerk.

At the end of October I heard through the 'grapevine' that the NAAFI in Bari had some cases of 20,000 English cigarettes available, all quite legitimate - so I persuaded my officer to advance me £50 and Bert and I went in to collect - it was all in order and this time I had someone to guard my precious load. We got back safely and I sold them to the lads (with a small profit to myself, of course). I was probably the most popular man in the platoon at the time.

One other incident I must record. One day Les had a most unusual detail from the Military Police - one 3-tonner and driver to report to a Pioneer unit in Bari at 4 o'clock in the morning. Dvr. Dodds ('Doddie') was sent and when he returned later that morning and told us all about it, I was so intrigued (if that is the word) that I asked Les, if it was ever repeated, would he send me? He agreed and on Nov. 18th an identical instruction came through and Les was as good as his word and I got the detail. I duly reported to 66 Group Pioneers at 4.45a.m. I picked up a captain, CSM and four pioneers who loaded a coffin, blankets, knives and hammers into my truck, for this was the execution of an Italian spy. We drove to a wadi well outside the city and were the first to arrive. There was a simple stand for use as a rifle rest, and facing it a rough wooden chair in front of a small wall of sandbags. At about 6 the main party arrives, a firing squad of twelve men, several military police with their officer, some American officers, some members of the Italian Caribinieri and lastly the prisoner, escorted by a CMP officer and a priest. The firing squad line up, the spy, dressed in civilian clothes with a large white patch on his chest, is taken to the chair and bound to it and a black bag is placed over his head. The priest murmurs a short prayer and moves away, an order is given, the man shouts 'Viva l'Italia', a volley rings out and the man slumps forward in the chair and it is all over. An officer then examines the body to ensure that he is dead - everyone now retires and the pioneers take the coffin down, place the body in it, while I back my truck down and the coffin is loaded into it. The Pioneer captain and the priest then get in the cab with me, while the other four ride in the back and we return to Bari and drive to the cemetary where the coffin is unloaded and the priest stays with it. We return to the Pioneer HQ where I am given a good breakfast and dismissed with the instruction to wash down the inside of my truck when I get back. It was an interesting if macabre experience, but I have always tried to see as much of life (and death) as possible, or perhaps it was just morbid curiosity.

The weather is now much colder, so I got my Italian 'odd job' man to build a fireplace in my office-cum-bedroom. December passes with the same old routines and Christmas Day saw the usual celebrations - an excellent meal and afterwards I sat in front of my new fire and wrote letters home. I have not said much about letters, but incoming mail was always the high spot of the day and writing letters home took up a considerable amount of time. After the letters I went to the canteen for tea and cakes and was guard commander at 6.30 p.m.

Here I must introduce a couple who became our very good friends - they were Egon and Hilda Domac, a married couple who had escaped across the Adriatic from Split in Yugoslavia - he was a Slav from Zagreb and she an Austrian from Vienna and they had married just before the war. Both were excellent linguists, in addition to their mother tongue they also spoke English and Italian. They had rented a flat quite near to us in San Spirito and to Les and myself it became home from home - we spent most of our free evenings with them, playing bridge or talking, mostly about politics. Egon had a job with AMGOT while 'Bunny', as we called her, stayed at home and looked after the flat. We often had our evening meal with them and helped out with the occasional tin of something. I was also able to let them have a few things from my NAAFI store, such as soap and chocolate. Bunny had a brother who had emigrated to Kenya with his family before the war and had become a naturalised Britisher, and it was Egon and Bunny's ambition to join them there. They told us something of the terrible time they had suffered in Split under the Italians before they had made their escape.

1945

Another new year and, although the advance in Europe seems to be going well, there still seems no sign of the end of the war yet. I helped Egon draft his letter applying for their immigration permit - although his English is very good, he is always trying to improve and we have many discussions about English grammar - one phrase he could never get right was one we use constantly - 'what is the news?' - he could not understand why the word 'news' was singular - it has an 's' on the end, so it must be plural, so his daily greeting was always, "Hello Arthur, what are the news?" - it became a standing joke between us. Les or I could usually arrange transport for them in and out of Bari for shopping etc.

On February 11th we are at their flat as usual and we all drink to Michael, who is three today, and to my safe return. Again at the flat on March 1st we celebrate with a special meal and drink Sheila's health on our fourth wedding anniversary.

On March 11th we made our next move, after many months in San Spirito; luckily to a place not far away called Palese. This coincides with a complete reorganisation of our platoon, which is to become all-Italian under the administration of an English staff. Half of our drivers are to be transferred to 'A' platoon and the other half to 'C' platoon. (Our two Duck platoons have long since left us permanently). Fifteen of us including Les and myself will remain in 'B' to organise the Italians, not a job I relish. Our new billet at Palese is not nearly as comfortable as the ones at San Spirito, but no doubt we shall make improvements. Les and I and three other lads share one room - it is not far from San Spirito, and we can easily organise transport, so we are still able to see Egon and Bunny quite regularly.

On March 19th on my return from Bari about 5 o'clock, I am told that from tomorrow I am being attached as a clerk to CRASC (Commandant RASC), 12 General Transport Column, stationed in Bari. CRASC is the next higher echelon in the army hierarchy and the CO, a colonel, controls all RASC units in his area. Much as I would prefer to stay with the lads, there is nothing I can do

Egon.

Bunny.

about it, so next morning I pack my small kit and at 8 o'clock 'Doddie' takes me in the 15 cwt. to my new abode. I meet Johnnie Williams who has been on detachment from 72 Coy. before me and he puts me in the picture about my new routine. He returns to the unit a couple of days later. The staff under the colonel consists of an RSM (Regimental Sergeant Major) one staff sergeant, three full corporals and four clerks. The HQ is in a lovely old house about two miles outside Bari and very comfortable, though the sleeping quarters are a bit crowded, but they seem a decent bunch. We all eat in an NCO's mess, where we sit at a long table and very well cooked meals are served to us by an orderly - all very civilised. There is also a bar and table tennis, one of my weaknesses, so it won't be too bad. We keep civilian office hours except if on night duty, so I can still arrange to get out to San Spirito fairly frequently, thanks to Les, who arranged transport either with 'Doddie' in his 15 cwt, or on the back of a bike. The work is all clerical, mostly typing and dealing with returns and statistics coming in from all the RASC units in the area. So no more driving for me at present. I am up at 7 o'clock next morning after a cup of tea in bed!!! Towards the end of March we hear the news that the Russians are fighting in Berlin and expect to link up with the Americans hourly, which cheers us up greatly.

On April 9th there is a fearful explosion in Bari docks - an ammunition ship containing two hundred and fifty 500 lb. bombs blows up; all our windows two miles from the docks are shattered and a great column of smoke rises over the city. I went into Bari later and the damage is terrible, glass everywhere and many people killed. The remains of the ship are towed out to sea later in the afternoon. Tragically an almost identical explosion happened in December 1943 when we were in Naples, so of course we didn't know anything about it. That one was by enemy action. Again I quote from Churchill, Volume V, page 225.

"…a very damaging surprise attack on our crowded harbour of Bari on December 2nd blew up an ammunition ship with a chance hit and caused the sinking of sixteen other ships and the loss of 30,000 tons of cargo."

Bunny.

Bunny and Les.

Bunny and Doddie.

That was an unexpected air raid by a few German bombers, but this time it was an accident, as there are no raids now. I went out to San Spirito later and saw Les, Egon and Bunny. In my new routine I get a full day off once a week, something I have never had before.

News on April 27th that the Americans and Russians have linked up and that Mussolini has been captured by the Italian partisans and taken to Milan and shot, together with his mistress, and their bodies hung at a petrol station in the city. The allied armies are sweeping through northern Italy, so it looks as if things are beginning to move at last. The last few days in April and the beginning of May saw many rumours of the imminent collapse of Germany and the surrender to the allies - but the really exciting news came on May 2nd, with the announcement of the surrender of all German forces in Italy to General Alexander and the 'cease fire' from midday today. My diary records that 'the final collapse of Germany and the link-up with the Russians at many points culminated with the final surrender to 'Monty' on May 5th.' Although very remote from the European theatre, we followed events closely and would never miss a news broadcast - but in the meantime we carried on with our daily work.

Prior to those eventful days, I had been studying for and finally passed an exam on transport administration in the RASC - this made no difference to my 'way of life', but it did mean an increase in my pay, as I am now mustered as a Trade Tested Clerk.

On May 7th we heard that Churchill had announced the end of the war in Europe and that tomorrow, May 8th, would be 'VE' day - news we have all been waiting to hear for nearly six years.

I was on duty that night and, after breakfast and the 6.30 news bulletin, I arranged with Les for 'Doddie' to collect me at 4 o'clock. I went into Bari in the morning, bought some gloves for Sheila, had coffee and cakes at the Corner House, had a bath and haircut and went back to the Mess for lunch. I wrote some letters and heard Churchill's speech at 3 o'clock, then met 'Doddie', who took me out to Bunny and Egon's where Les was waiting. The four of us celebrated the end of the war, a day that it had seemed at times would never arrive. After an excellent meal we played games, talked a lot and finally at about 11 o'clock went for a walk along the seafront - it was all so peaceful it was hard to imagine that there had ever been a war. Les ran me back to my HQ in Bari in the water tanker at about 2 a.m.

After that momentous day things settled back to normal - one thing now dominated everyone's thoughts - Release - This was very fairly based on two factors, age and service - from these two figures every man had a release number, the lower the better - mine was 23, which was quite good. Later on when release started, dates for each group were published, starting with the lowest, and when a man's number 'came up' he would leave his unit and start his long journey home. Later on our unit became closely involved in this process, but at present all that is still a long way off, but at least it gave us something tangible to look forward to.

May and June passed uneventfully and, in spite of all my machinations, I am still at CRASC - I still manage regular visits to San Spirito until July 3rd when I learn from Les that 72nd Coy. is going to move again. I redouble my efforts to return and am finally successful and rejoin Les and the lads at Palese - Les is trying to arrange for Bunny and Egon to travel north with us, quite illegal in normal circumstances, but by now they are well known and liked in our platoon, so we hope that he will be successful.

July 3rd is also Margaret and Duncan's wedding day and letters from the family tell me that it is quite a big affair with about fifty guests. I feel very sad not to be with them, but I am thinking about them, as I am sure they will be thinking of me.

On July 8th, on the eve of our departure I am guard commander so get no sleep. Reveille is at 2.30 a.m. - Egon and Bunny have got permission to travel with us and arrive - we are all loaded up and move off at 4 o'clock. We are in 'Doddie's truck, 'Waf' Turner in the front, with Bunny and Egon, Les and myself in the back with the stores. We had a good run via Foggia to Naples and on to Nola, where we spend the night, Bunny sleeping in the back of the truck and the rest of us outside. During the night some Italians try to raid our cookhouse, but are driven off by shots from our guard. Our trucks had been carrying flour which was off-loaded the next day and we took on board a load of rations.

On July 11th we left and continued north passing the Anzio battlefield on the way and then on through Rome. We saw St. Peter's and the Vatican but didn't stop and parked up north of the 'Holy City' - north again on the 12th to Grossetto arriving about 2 o'clock. On again the next day to Leghorn and yet again on the 13th to Genoa. On the latter stages of this long trek north we see the results of the fierce fighting during the last stages of the Italian campaign. Every bridge is down, many replaced by the famous Bailey Bridge erected by the Engineers. We reach Genoa at about 2 o'clock on the 14th. After parking in some large barracks, the four of us go into the town and what a contrast! We have a very good meal at a 'posh' restaurant and my diary reads - "This town is wonderful, really civilised and the people very smart and well dressed - shops well stocked, street lighting, traffic lights and trams. All very bewildering after our long sojourn in the wilds of Southern Italy."

The next day we pressed on to our final destination, Milan, having travelled the full length of Italy in just a week. We dropped Bunny and Egon off to find a room for themselves and we then move to our new billet, all together in a large block of buildings - we collect a lot of back mail and settle down for a good night's sleep.

Northern Italy

Next day, July 16th, after a parade at 8.30 we settled into our new quarters, pulling down a 'blast' wall and moving the stores into our new offices. Bunny and Egon have found a nice flat near the Cathedral and the following day Les, Doddie and I moved all their luggage into their new home, climbing up 94 stairs. It is very comfortable, and they were lucky to have found somewhere so quickly - we had the rest of the day free, so wrote letters and visited the NAAFI.

By now release is starting for the lower numbers and Milan is the 'jumping off' point for all troops stationed in Italy. There are two centres in the area, a Transit Camp, where new arrivals congregate first and then move on to the Release Assembly Area, where all kit deficiencies are made up, medical inspections, travel warrants and release documents issued and any pay queries sorted out. All this takes from 24 to 48 hours. From here they are taken to the main station in Milan, from where they start the long train journey home. 72 Coy's role is again troop-carrying, ferrying servicemen and women between these three points. So the unit has come full circle and has now reverted to the original troop-carrying role for which it was originally formed in Southport in 1939. Luckily for us, this also means that we are ideally situated for a quick get-away when our numbers come up for release.

The next week was spent getting to know our way around and finding the many Service Clubs in Milan - it is very hot and we patronise the local swimming pool. On July 31st I am told that I am to be detached to CRASC, yet again, this time to 78 General Transport Column based in Milan. I hate the idea and see Capt. Emmerson, my platoon officer, and also the CO, but to no avail; so next morning Doddie takes me to CRASC at 9 o'clock. This one is also situated in a big house in a built-up area on the outskirts of the city. I have an interview with the Adjutant, Capt. Piper, a very decent chap, who is sympathetic, but wants to keep me - I am put in charge of their domestic transport, so it may not be too bad. I am on duty that evening. A little later I have another interview with the Adjutant and am now doing 'Q' duties in addition to transport.

Sunday, August 5th was a free day, so myself and two other clerks take a 15 cwt. truck (with permission) and spent the day at Como. It was very pleasant - we sat by the lake and then drove some way along the lakeside. On our return to Como we parked the truck and went up the famous funicular railway to Brunate at the summit. We had tea and cakes at the Blue Lagoon (NAAFI) and got back to Milan about 8 o'clock after a very good day out.

I was getting very fed up at this time and put in an application to revert to Driver, and on Aug. 9th I reported sick complaining of acute depression. The MO asked me a lot of irrelevant questions and then recommended me for local leave. The next day I had an interview with the Colonel, who was very decent and granted me six days leave and asked me to "Go away for a week, forget the whole matter and on your return I hope you will feel better" - so that is what I did. I had an FFI (Free from Infection) medical that morning, saw Bunny and Egon and told them of my new plans, and caught the 4 o'clock train for the Rest Camp at Como. The train was most luxurious, the first time I had been on one since leaving England and it reminded me of the many times I had 'trained' between Ascot and London. At Como I walked to 58 Rest Camp, which is a civilian holiday complex taken over by the British Services - my room is very comfortable with bathroom 'en suite'. I have my evening meal in a communal dining hall, but with individual tables set with white linen cloths, cutlery, cup and saucer. There are rolls and butter and tea in a real pot. Italian waitresses serve the food and that first night we had soup, roast beef and Yorkshire pudding, baked potatoes, onions, runner beans, followed by fruit tart with condensed milk - I think I am going to enjoy my week here!! The bed is not very comfortable and I wish I had brought my Lilo - the 'mattress' is wooden slats, so I end up on the floor. Italian maids look after the rooms so there are no duties whatsoever. On Aug. 11th came the news of the Japanese surrender, but I don't suppose it will make any difference to our release dates. One of the highlights of my week was a more leisurely trip up the funicular. This time I was able to go into the tower and climb the 143 steps to the top - the view is really superb, with Como below and the lake stretching away to the north as far as the eye can see. In the evening, before coming down, I walked to the Italian/Swiss frontier, marked by a high wire fence. By now it was dusk and looking down on the Swiss side I could see the myriad of lights of the town of Chiasso nestling in the valley - it is strange when one realises that those same lights have been shining all through the past six dreadful years, while the rest of Europe was plunged in black-outs and bombings - the Swiss certainly do have something! On my way down the funicular the driver showed me his cab and the control room, all spotless and beautifully maintained. I returned to camp after a really good day. I spent some time on the lake, hiring a boat and sunbathing - I also tried my hand at fishing, but without success. There is also an indoor swimming pool which I enjoy. One day I took a bus to Chiasso, but at the frontier an Italian soldier tells me I have to get off, so I walk along the fence for some way and then get a bus back. On my fourth day I caught a very fast train back to Milan - I did some shopping, called to see Bunny and Egon and took her to the pictures. After tea I caught a very slow and crowded train back to Como, but this time I had to ride in the goods truck. I also took a trip on the lake on a paddle steamer, visiting Menaggio and Bellagio - I also visited Como zoo. After a very pleasant and relaxed week I returned to CRASC on Friday, August 17th. I learned that there has been a speed-up in release dates and, on the present schedule, I could be home by November 25th. I settled

58 Rest Camp - Como.

back in and wrote some letters.

September arrived and with it the sixth anniversary of the outbreak of war, followed on the 15th by my own joining-up anniversary, but this time the war is over and it is just a matter of 'marking time' until my magic number comes up.

I have met up with Bert again and we spend much of our spare time together. We see a lot of films and spend time at the various servicemen's clubs that seem to abound, and play table tennis.

On Sept. 11th I am told that I have to move into the company office and a Sgt. Bumpus is to take over my stores. The office routine is much the same as at CRASC, Bari - our work consists mainly of receiving 'vehicle available' states from units and then matching them up against demands for transport from depots, dumps, transit centres and so on. We still keep office hours, apart from the occasional night duty, so I am able to see Bunny and Egon at their flat fairly often, but transport is more strictly controlled, so I have to use the trams.

On Oct. 9th it is officially published that release for my group 23 will commence on Dec. 7th so with luck, I could be home for Christmas. Since returning from Como I have had a bedroom to myself, but a new CSM arrives and commandeers it for himself, so I have to move in with Johnnie Williams.

About this time a 5-day course in Rome is advertised on our notice board. The subject is 'The Historical Background to Roman Civilisation' to commence on October 22nd. It sounds deadly dull, but we rushed through Rome on our way north and this seems to be my only chance to see the city, so I applied for a vacancy. Somewhat to my surprise the Adjutant agreed to let me go. So on the afternoon of Oct. 20th, a truck took me to Novara station 45 miles from Milan. I reported to the RTO (Railway Transport Office), but my train was several hours late - eventually it arrived - it is a passenger troop train with hard wooden seats and I share a compartment with three RAF lads and an RA sergeant. The train left just before midnight and we arrived at Bologna about 8.30 next morning and stopped for breakfast - on again to Rimini on the Adriatic coast about midday for a meal. We got to Spolletta about 8 o'clock for another hot meal, finally reaching Rome at 1 o'clock in the morning. I noted that by road

Como.

the journey from Milan is about 450 miles, but by the troop train running in conjunction with leave and release, it is almost 800. But I must say the meals at all the stops were extremely well organised. On arrival at Rome station I rang the camp and they sent a staff car to collect me and I bedded down about 2 a.m.

The course is organised by the Army Education Corps and we are housed in some Italian barracks. As the course does not start until tomorrow, I have a free day - I walk round this bit of Rome and see some of the sights, have a tour in the military bus and visit the YMCA canteen, then back to the billet, wrote some letters and so to bed. The course proper started next morning and there are only about a dozen of us, including one officer and four ATS girls. We have lectures in the mornings by an ex-Cooks Tour Guide and after lunch are taken by him in a special coach to see the 'sights' - St. Peter's and the Sistine Chapel, including a climb up into the dome, the Vatican Museum, the Forum, the Colosseum, Borghese Galleries, Baths of Caracalla and the Catacombs. We also had a lecture on 'The Rise of Papacy' by a Russian lady and on another day a talk on Italian Opera at the Rome Arts Club, illustrated by records. We also had a talk by a Miss Garibaldi on the life of her famous grandfather. In the evenings we were free and visited the many clubs and canteens and as usual saw some films.

One special event happened on our last day, an audience with

The Rome Tour Group.

the Pope - of course there were hundreds present - we gathered in the Audience Chamber, one end of which was roped off and guarded by the Swiss Guards in their traditional uniforms - at precisely midday the Pope arrived attended by several Cardinals and other Vatican officials. He took his place and welcomed us to the Vatican in several languages and then pronounced his Blessing and withdrew and we filed out into St Peter's Square. A truly memorable occasion although I am not a Catholic. The course ended on October 29th and the next day I reported to Movement Control for my return. We went in a very crowded TCV (Troop Carrying Vehicle) via Perugia and Arezzo to Florence, arriving about 6.15 p.m., where I reported to the Transit Camp and arranged to stay over the next day. I had coffee and sandwiches at the S.A. club and then had a good night's sleep. Next day I had to stay in camp until midday, but then visited the Cathedral, and spent some time there and also saw several of the Art Galleries. Later I had a meal at the Robertson Club, saw a show and went back to camp. On Nov. 1st, I was on a truck going to Bologna - after a very rough journey I reported to the Reception Centre about midday. The rest of the day was free and I am due to catch a train to Milan at 9 p.m. Of course it was late and eventually left about midnight. It was packed with servicemen and women, all travelling on LIAP (something to do with leave, but I've forgotten what the letters stand for) and release. We crossed the river Po on a very unstable temporary bridge and reached Milan about 7 a.m. Altogether a wonderful week, far more interesting and instructive than I had thought it would be.

Things soon settled back to normal - I visited Bunny and Egon, went to the Victory Club with Bert, played table tennis, etc. On November 7th, I am told that we are moving to Genoa tomorrow. I am not at all happy about this, as it means I am one step further away from the Release Centre and shall also lose touch with Bunny and Egon, also Les and Bert. However there is nothing I can do about it. We left at 11.30 with me travelling in the back of a QL lorry with all the stationery. We have to make a long detour owing to floods and arrive about 5.30 after a terrible journey, so, after unloading, I went to bed. I am billeted with another lad and the CRASC office is 10 minutes' walk away. There are civilian clerks and we spent the next day sorting out stores and settling in.

The next three weeks were entirely uneventful - the office routine continues and I go out with some of the lads from the office, the usual round of films, clubs and walks round Genoa. The only bright spot (and how bright it is) is the thought that my release is only a matter of days away. On November 21st, my release book is collected from area HQ. Towards the end of the month I begin to panic - CRASC won't release me until a replacement arrives, so on the 27th I get in touch with 72 Coy. at Milan and am told that they are sending a clerk called Adamson to take my place tomorrow and I am to return the following day - so far so good. But when tomorrow comes I hear that Adamson is not coming after all and that a chap called Jenkins is coming from 59 area HQ - panic again, and my diary reads 'I am watching things very closely'. On Thursday Nov. 29th S/Sgt Robb phones to say that he hopes Jenkins will be leaving today - I ring Jenkins at Area HQ and he says he knows nothing about any move - panic again. I told Capt. Stevens and asked if I could return to Milan tomorrow, but when he spoke to the Major about it he (the Major) said that any day up to Dec. 14th was OK - maybe for them, but not for me. I was determined to spend this Christmas with my family. I learn that the Colonel is travelling to Milan on Sat. Dec. 1st, and I get permission to travel with him. I repack my kit in preparation for my departure. The Colonel is due to leave in the afternoon, but on the Friday I hear that he may not be going until Sunday - panic again. I found out that a lorry is leaving for Milan the next morning, and I arranged with the driver to hang on until I see whether I can get permission to travel with him. I ask Capt. Stevens and he gives his permission. (I have to restrain myself from embracing him!!!) I dash back to my billet, collect my kit and hurl it into the back of the waiting truck and we are away. I ride in the back and it is very cold, but who cares! I arrive at 72 Coy. at 1.30 and report to S/Sgt Robb, who says I can leave for the Assembly Area today. (as we are in Milan, we do not need to go to a Transit Camp). I rang Egon and arranged a meeting and by 4 o'clock I am at 20 Assembly Area - it is a vast place with a staff of 2,000 but the organisation is perfect. At reception my index card is extracted from a file and in five minutes I am 'IN' - I meet up with the other lads in group 23 from 72 Coy. and as we are not 'confined to barracks' I went into Milan to a club, wrote my last letter home, and met Bunny and Egon at their flat - they were very pleased to see me after such a long time and happy at the prospect of my return home. I gave them my parting gifts I bought in Genoa - we had a farewell meal at their flat and I returned to the Assembly Area at 11.30.

Next day, Sunday, Dec 2nd, I messed about the camp all morning, bought some more presents at the camp Gift Shop, then went into Milan again. I had some tea at the Club and rang Bunny and arranged to spend my last evening with them. I got to their flat about 7 and we had coffee and talked and I said my final goodbyes and left about 10 o'clock.

Before we bid a final farewell to Egon and Bunny there is one incident I must relate that happened shortly after I got home. I had always thought that Egon was involved in some shady dealings since he landed in Italy (who wasn't?), but he never talked about it. And after all, they had escaped from Split with only the clothes they stood up in. Egon also knew that I had made the odd lira here and there. Some time early in 1946 when we were all living in Birmingham with my parents while waiting for our flat to be finished, I had a mysterious letter from Egon, still in Milan, in which he mentioned that he was sending me 'five hundred pairs of silk stockings', and that more would follow, and would I keep them for him? This baffled us until, a short time later, a man called and handed me a package - he had a taxi waiting and before I could question him, he was gone. When we opened the parcel we found it contained one hundred five pounds notes - then the penny dropped - Egon was trying to get some of his money out of Italy through the UK. My parents were shocked - £500 was a large amount in those days and I too didn't want to get involved in anything shady now that I was back in 'civvie street'. It was obvious that Egon was breaking the strict exchange control regulations that were in force at that time. So I wrote back at once saying I was very sorry, but I could not help him, and he must relieve me of the 'silk stockings' urgently. He replied, apologising, and a little later I had a phone call from a lady in London, who asked me if I had a package from Italy for her. I said yes, and, as she couldn't get to Birmingham, she asked me if I could meet her in London to hand the package over to her. Naturally I agreed and it was arranged that we would meet in the foyer of the Strand Palace Hotel at a certain time on a certain date. We also agreed a means of mutual identification. (Talk about a 'cloak and dagger' operation). I travelled to London by train with the 'stockings', met her as arranged and we went into the lounge. She was a charming lady and over tea we talked and I handed her the package and asked her if she wanted to check it, but she said no, she was sure it was all right. I got her to sign a receipt for it and we parted and that is really the end of the story.

I kept in touch with Bunny and Egon for some time after I returned home - I know they did manage to get to Kenya where later I believe Egon had some heart trouble - but over the years we lost touch - a great pity, because they were a delightful couple and very hospitable both in San Spirito and Milan.

But back to the Assembly Area. On my return that night I learn that I am on a draft leaving at 5 a.m. next morning. I snatch a few hours' sleep and am awakened by loudspeaker at 4 a.m. We parade with our kit and are taken by truck (72 Coy.) to Milan station, where a special platform is reserved for the troop trains taking release personnel on the long journey across Europe. We are escorted from the trucks to the train by Military Police. The train leaves at 7 a.m. We are seven to a compartment, which is very comfortable with heating. (It is a very cold, wet morning). We reach Domodossola, just south of the frontier at 11.15, where there is a hot meal waiting. Then on through the Simplon Tunnel and into Switzerland, along the shores of a lake to Lucerne, where we are greeted over the loudspeakers with a 'bon voyage', then across Switzerland and over the frontier into France. We eat our haversack rations and arrive at Dijon at 9.30 p.m., where another meal is waiting for us. Afterwards we settle down to get some sleep, while the train continues on through the night. Next morning we have some breakfast and are given English newspapers, also some more haversack rations. Then on through Creil and Boves, by-passing Paris, and arrive at Amiens during the afternoon. It is now very cold and the heating has gone off (trust the French) - we finally arrive at Calais about 7.30 p.m. - we walk the short distance to 112 Transit Camp where a loud-speaker tells us to collect one blanket. We are then taken to hut 49 and after a hot meal we bed down for the night, and my diary reads 'my last night overseas'.

On Dec. 5th we parade at 9 o'clock and are driven in trucks to the docks and go aboard the good old 'Lady of Man' (which revives memories of October 1939), and she sails at 11 o'clock.

I stayed on deck, not wishing to miss my first glimpse of dear old England. It was cold and windy, but not very rough. I got a lump in my throat when I first saw the white cliffs of Dover and we docked at 11.45 and adjusted our watches by one hour. We went ashore and left by train about 1. We went through Ashford, Tonbridge, Redhill, Reigate and Dorking and arrived at Aldershot about teatime, where a truck takes us to a barracks. An officer then tells us that we will be demobilised here and we will draw civilian clothes tomorrow - we are shown our billet, have a hot meal and spend the rest of the evening talking.

Next day, Thursday, December 6th, is the day I have been waiting for, for six long years, my last in the army. At 8 o'clock we are called by loudspeaker and after breakfast we parade with personal kit. From there we are taken to a large hall and then it is just a matter of moving from one counter to another, each one dealing with one piece of equipment which we hand over and lastly our final documentation. We are then taken by truck to a civilian clothing depot at Woking, where we are issued with our 'demob suit' and then we are free to walk away from the Army.

Outside I say goodbye to the other chaps and catch a train to London, where I ring Sheila to tell her I am home and to confirm our arrangements. After so long away, both Sheila and I wanted a few hours to ourselves before I was 'submerged' by my family, so she had booked a room at the Lygon Arms Hotel at Broadway in the Cotswolds. At Paddington I had a wash and brush-up in the cloakroom and caught the 4.45 train to Broadway. And it was there at the Lygon Arms that I finally met up with my Sheila after two years, seven months and thirty days separation.

How do I sum up a slice of over six years taken out of my life? Apart from the long separation from Sheila and Michael and up until March 1945, I enjoyed my army life - it had its ups and downs and I enjoyed the action and the driving, especially my time with the Ducks; but I found the last ten months when I was at CRASC tedious and boring in the extreme - I had no opportunity to drive or ride - it was all desk work, but this period was certainly helped by the kindness of Bunny and Egon, who made this period of my army life bearable: and of course for the first time I could see that the war was ending and that release was shining at the end of the long, dark tunnel.

Epilogue

And so this unexpected episode in my life comes to an end. As things turned out, my civilian job at the outbreak of the war in 1939 became a 'reserved occupation', and I could have spent all the war years at home - however, looking back, I would not have missed the excitement and the experience for anything. There was heart-break and sadness in plenty, first and foremost being the separation from Sheila and Michael for nearly three years, but of course it was being in the army that brought us together in the first place.

I was very lucky that, like my father, I survived unscathed and also I managed to stay with the same unit throughout and so made many very good friends. My one regret is that, apart from Jack Browne, I have lost touch with the 'lads' who shared the war years with me - as I explained in Chapter 1, they came mostly from Lancashire, and we have lived in Reigate for the last 39 years, but perhaps through Jack, who still lives in Southport, some of them may read this and perhaps it will bring back some memories for them as re-writing my diaries has for me.

1996